The Second Coming Of Jesus Christ

Bishop Emmanuel Boachie

Printed in the U.S.A
Copyright © 2017
Bishop Emmanuel Boachie
All rights reserved solely by the author. The author guarantees all contents are original and do not infringe upon legal rights of any other person or work. No part of this book may be reproduced in any form except for brief quotations in printed reviews, without the permission of the author

Unless otherwise stated, all Scripture quotations are taken from the *Holy Bible*, King James Version *(KJV)*
ISBN-13: 978-0997621358
ISBN-10: 0997621354

Dedication

This special book is dedicated to the Holy Spirit who is my special teacher, Jesus said in the book of John 14:26 But the Comforter, which is the Holy Ghost, whom the Father will send in my name, he shall teach you all things, and bring all things in remembrance, whatsoever I have said unto you. And also to my beloved wife Prophetess Deborah Boachie, who can find a virtuous wife? For her worth is far above rubies. The heart of the husband safely trust her, so he will have no lack of gain (See Prov. 31:10-11). And all believers who are fully dedicated their lives to God, and his work that very soon our Lord Jesus Christ will come, and judge the whole world in truth, the word of God says, and as it is appointed unto men only to die once, but after this the judgment. Hebrews 9:27. If you be ashamed to mention His Name He too, will be ashamed to mention your name to His Father, when he comes in the glory of his Father in the presence of the holy Angels in heaven. If you have every good thing in this world, such as houses, cars, money, live stocks, and companies and you did not accept Jesus Christ as your personal savor, you will die and go to hell. All your possessions cannot save your life.

If you seek for God you will find him, brethren dedicate your entire life to God once you are still alive, you cannot accept or dedicate your life to God when you die, and you need to do it today.

Acknowledgement

First of all, I acknowledge and give thanks to the God of heaven and earth who is the Captain of my life, The Trinity, God the Father, who is the Father of our Lord Jesus Christ. God the Son, who is my Lord and Savior Jesus Christ, the Captain of my soul and God the Holy Spirit, my Master and Teacher who has performed a great work concerning this book, all thanks be ascribed to the Most High God, Almighty and the Everlasting God, who gave me this opportunity to write this important book the mystery of the end time with full of information concerning the rapture of the church, the reign of the Antichrist, The war of the Armageddon and the Second Coming of our Lord Jesus Christ, for His revelations, wisdom and understanding given from above to publish this book.

Secondly, my gratitude and thanks goes to my beloved wife, Prophetess Mrs. Deborah Boachie, my better half, and the honey of my life. I thank the Lord that He gave you to me. You are a virtuous woman, whom I appreciate so much since you became my wife, your encouragement, prayers, support, advice, sleepless nights sitting with me in bringing and knocking the pieces of this book together. Indeed, the Bible says he who finds a wife, has found a good thing, and have obtained favor in the sight of God. May the good God bless you with great reward (favor). I also appreciate my children: Pastor Richard Amoah, Mrs. Rachel Amoah Ofosu, Rev Enos Opoku Boateng, Mrs. Priscilla Boachie Ofori, Edmund Donkor, Mrs Marie Quansah and Emmanuella Pomaah Boachie. My prayer for you is that, God Almighty will help all of you, to fulfill your dreams in Jesus name.

Thirdly, I appreciate the entire congregation of Jesus Power Redemption Ministry, United States of America, and New Covenant Life Chapel. The families that have been concerned, lovely, and have shown kindness to me and my family. Mr. & Mrs. Anthony Agblevor and family. Rev and Mrs. Benjamin and Mrs Judith Boakye & family, Ebenezer Assembly of God family, may the God Almighty bless you in Jesus name.

God bless my son in law Deacon Kojo Ofori for his prayers and his words of encouragement. I appreciate and thank God for Jesus Power prayer ministry for your love, prayers and the support you gave to me. Rev. and Mrs. Ben Ankomah, God bless you so much, he who sees your good work in secret will surely reward you openly. I'm very grateful for everything you did for me when I came to you in North Carolina. You showed me love and kindness. No wonder God is lifting you up to higher grounds for you to become an Immigration Officer, in United States of America, God bless you and your family in Jesus name.

Finally I appreciate Nana Owusu Manu, for the great work done, calling you all the time. Nana thanks for your time spent, the encouragement, and the love. I know for sure it will not be in vain. May your going out and coming in be a blessing. I sincerely thank Rev Dr Pauline Walley Daniels and Rev Dr Kissi Peprah for helping to proofreading and editing. of this book. For all the time and resources lost on my behalf, I pray the Lord God restores it back to you beyond measure. I thank God for the life of Mr. and Mrs. Richard Adjei who helped and, supported me and gave me a place to stay with them, fed me, showed me kindness and love, when I came from North Carolina to New York State, in fact they were the first faces I saw in New York. Thank you so much that you allowed the God of heaven to use you, God bless you. I thank God Almighty, for your life that the love between us is growing from grace to grace. May the God of eternity bless you and all the family, I will always remember what you have done, and my prayer is that what you have done for me should be a memorial in God's presence all day-long thank you. How can I forget to appreciate Mr. Junior Taveras and Mr. Helky Taveras for the great job which they offered to me by doing the typesetting, causing you sleepless nights, your labor will surely not be in van may the Almighty God bless the work of your hand. Rev and Mrs Joseph Kuffour, and the Inspiration Gospel Assembly family, may the God of heaven bless you for the great work offered. Thank you so much for allowing God Almighty to use you for this great book.

Email: bishopboachie83@gmail.com
boachieyiadom83@yahoo.com
Mobile Phones: 929-360-6940
347-259-1172
718-503-2280
Website: http//www.bishopemmanuelboachie.com
Bishop Emmanuel Boachie is a member of Faithful Ministers Fellowship (FMF)

Table of Contents

The First Coming of Our Lord Christ Jesus.   1

The Calculations of Prophet Daniel's Vision.   13

The Interpretations on the Second Coming of Christ. 21

What Is The Cross And Why Did He Died On The Cross? 23

The Cross and the Christians.   29

What Is The Permanent Resurrection?   49

What Are The Qualifications Of Rapture?   59

Events in Heaven and Earth That Will Follow Rapture. 65

Events That Will Take Place between Rapture And Revelation.   81

The Conquer Of Many Nations. 93

The Two Witnesses and Their Mission.   99

The Time and Length of the Tribulation. 109

Antichrist, the King of The North And His Functions. 123

Reasons Why Russian Is Not the King of the North. 131

The Divisions of the Tribulation 135

Jesus Rose from the Dead for Us 139

The Resurrection of the Dead and the Final Judgment. 143

What Is Faithfulness In Service? 155

The Reasons Why One Hundred And Forty Four Thousand Are The Man Child. 169

Will The Rapture Of The Church Happen First Before The Reveal Of The Antichrist? 191

Chapter One

The First Coming of Our Lord Christ Jesus.

The coming of the Messiah, was first announced in the book of Genesis chapter three verse fifteen which states, "And I will put enmity between you and the woman, and between your offspring and her offspring, He will bruise and tread your head under foot, and you lie in wait and bruise His heel" (Amplified Bible). The human race started with Adam and Eve, God gave them a commandment in Genesis 2:16-17,

> And the Lord God commanded the man, saying, you can freely eat of every tree of the garden, But of the tree of the knowledge of good and evil and blessing and calamity you shall not eat, for the day that you eat of it you shall surely die.

The temptation and the fall of man as recorded in the book of Genesis chapter three, Bible says,

> Now the serpent was more cunning than any beast of the field which the Lord God had made. And he said to the woman, has God indeed said, you shall not eat of every tree of the garden? And the woman said to the serpent, We may eat the fruit of the trees of the garden, but of the fruit of the tree which is in the midst of the garden, God has said, You shall not eat of it, nor shall you touch it, least you die. Then the serpent said to the woman, you will not surely die. For God knows that in the day you eat of it your eyes will be opened, and will be like God, knowing good and evil.' So when the woman saw that the tree was good for food, that it was pleasant

to the eyes, and the tree desirable to make one wise, she took of its fruit and ate. She also gave to her husband with her, and he ate.

Scriptures says that because of Adam and his wife's disobedience, they lost the glory that God gave to them and it was then that man die, and the fellowship between God and man came to an end. Then God Almighty gave the first prophecy concerning the First coming of our Lord Jesus who would come to the earth to restore the lost glory, to bring back the keys which Satan had taken from Adam and Eve, God said and I will put enmity between you (serpent) and the woman, between your seed Satan, and her seed Christ the Messiah the mediator between God and man, the one who can die for mankind to offer Himself as sacrifice for the sin which man committed in the garden of Eden. That very sin, man cannot do anything about it so God had to send His only begotten Son to come as an expiation for the sin of mankind. The scripture states that, "For the wages of sin is death but the gift of God is everlasting life through Jesus Christ our Lord." (Romans 6:23.)

The first Adam and his wife disobeyed God's commandment and they were deceived by Satan.

The seed of Satan is the serpent. "You shall bruise His heel," really happened on the cross of Calvary. Jesus was crucified on the cross and died on the cross. Satan actually was happy because of the death of Jesus Christ the Son of God. He was buried after His death, and the Bible says that Jesus went to hell to receive the keys which Satan took from Adam. Jesus Christ when He resurrected from death came to tell His disciples that all power in heaven and on earth had been given unto Him. (Matthew 28: 18).

In Galatians 4:4-6 it states,

"But when the fullness of the time had come, God sent forth His Son, born of woman, born under the law, to redeem those who were under the law, that we might receive the adoption as sons. And because you are sons God has sent forth the Spirit of His Son into your hearts, crying Abba Father. For God demonstrate His love towards us in that while we were still living in sin God sent His Son Jesus Christ to come and die for our sinners.

The coming of the Messiah was prophesy through many of the prophets, Moses the servant of God prophesied to the forefathers,

> The Lord God will raise up you, a prophet from among your brethren as He raised up me, Him you shall listen to and understand by hearing and heed in all things whatever He tells you. And it shall be that every soul that does not listen to and understand by hearing and heed that Prophet shall be utterly exterminated from among the people. (Deuteronomy18:15-19)

When we read Matthew 13:57 it states, "And they were offended in him. But Jesus said unto them a prophet is not without honor, save his country, and his own house." Moses told our forefathers that God will raise a Prophet up just as He raised him up, that anyone, they supposed to listen to Him and understand and be obedient to His sayings. Anyone who will disobey Him will be exterminated from among the people, therefore God is commanding all mankind to obey His beloved Son Jesus and have life.

ISAIAH PROPHESY FOR THE FIRST COMING OF THE MESSIAH

In the book of Isaiah chapter 7:14, the Bible says, "Therefore the Lord Himself will give you a sign, behold a virgin shall conceive and bear a Son, and shall call His name Immanuel."

The Prophecy came to pass in the book of Matthew chapter 1:20-23 which states,

> An angel of the Lord appeared to him in a dream, saying, Joseph, son of David, do not afraid to take to you Mary your wife, for that which is conceived in her is of the Holy Spirit. And she will bring forth a Son, and you shall call His name Jesus for He will save His people from their sins. So all this was done that it might be fulfilled which was spoken by the Lord through the Prophet, saying, Behold, the virgin shall be with child, and bear a Son, and they shall call His name Immanuel, which is translated, God with us.
>
> For unto us a Child is born, unto us a Son is given, and the government will be upon His shoulder. And His name will be called Wonderful, Counselor, Mighty God, Everlasting Father, Prince of Peace, of the increase of His government and peace, there will be no end, upon the throne of David and over His kingdom, to order it and establish it with judgment and justice from that time forward, even forever.
>
> The zeal of the Lord of hosts will perform this. (Isaiah 9:6-7)

The Prophet did not prophesy only about His birth but also His suffering and His death, His burial and His resurrection from death likewise.

> He is despised and rejected by men, A Man of sorrows And acquainted with grief. And we hid, as it were, our faces from Him, He was despised, and we did not esteem Him. Surely He has borne our grief and carried our sorrows, yet we esteemed Him stricken, smitten by God, and afflicted. But He was wounded for our transgressions, He was bruised for our iniquities, the

chastisement of our peace was upon Him, and by His stripes we are healed, all we like sheep have gone astray, we have turned, every one, to his own way, and Lord has laid on Him the iniquity of us all. He was oppressed and He was afflicted yet He opened not His mouth, He was led as a lamb to the slaughter, and as a sheep before its shearers is silent, so He opened not His mouth. He was taken from prison and from judgment, and who will declare His generation? For He was cut off from the land of living, for the transgressions of my people He was stricken. And they made His grave with the wicked but with the rich at His death. Because He had no violence not was any deceit in His mouth. Therefore I will divide Him a portion with the great, and He shall divide the spoil with the strong, because He poured out His soul unto death, and He was numbered with the transgressors, and He bore the sin of many, and made intercession for the transgressors.

God promised Abraham that the Messiah would come through his lineage in Genesis 12:1-3 which states, "Now the Lord said to Abram, get out of your country, from your family and from your father's house, to a land that I will show you. I will make you a great nation, I will bless you and make your name great and you shall be a blessing. I will bless those who bless you, and I will curse those who curse you, and in you all the families of the earth shall be blessed."
Now the Lord said to Abram: Get out of your country, from your family and from your father's house, to a land that I will show you. I will make you a great nation, and I will bless you, and make your name great, and you shall be a blessing. I will bless those who bless you, and I will curse those who curse you, and in you all the families of the earth shall be blessed. Jesus Christ the Messiah came through the lineage of Abraham, He

came through one of the twelve families called the tribe of Judah.

THE GOD WHO REVEALED DREAMS

You, O king, saw, and behold, there was a great image. This image was mighty and of exceedingly great brightness stood before you, and the appearance of it was frightening and terrible. As for this image, its head was of fine gold, its breast and its arms of silver, its belly and its thighs of bronze, its legs of iron, its feet partly of iron and partly of clay the baked clay of the potter. As you looked, a stone was cut out without human hands, which smote the image on its feet of iron and baked clay of the potter and broke them into pieces. Then the iron, the clay, the bronze, the silver, and the gold were broken and crushed together and became like a chaff of the summer threshing floors, and the wind carried them away so that not a trace of them could be found. And the stone that smote the image became a great mountain or rock and filled the whole earth. You O king, are king of the earthly king of whom the God of heaven has given the kingdom, the power, the might, and the glory. (Daniel 2: 31- 37, NKJV)
See Jeremiah 25:9-14,

> Behold I will send and take all the families of the north, says the Lord, and Nebuchadnezzar king of Babylon, My servant, and will bring them against this land, against its inhabitants, and against these nations all around, and will utterly destroyed them, and make them astonishment, a hissing, and perpetual desolations. Moreover, I will take from them the voice of mirth and the voice of gladness, the voice of bridegroom and the voice of bride, the sound of the milestones and the light of the lamp. And this whole land shall be a desolation and an astonishment, and these nations shall serve the king of Babylon seventy years. Then it will come to pass, when

seventy years are completed, that I will punish the king of Babylon and that nation, the land of the Chaldeans, for their iniquity, says the Lord, and I will make it a perpetual desolation. I will bring on that land all my words which I have pronounced against it, all that is written in the books, which Jeremiah has prophesied concerning all the nations. For many nations and great kings shall be served by them also, and I will repay them according to their deeds and according to the works of their own hands. And wherever the children of men dwell, and the beast of the field, and the birds of the heavens He has given them into your hand and has made you rule over them all. You king of Babylon are the head of gold. And after you shall arise another kingdom the Medo-Persian, inferior to you, and still a third kingdom of bronze Greece under Alexander the Great, which shall bear rule over all the earth. And the fourth kingdom Rome shall be strong as iron, since iron breaks to pieces and subdues all things, and like iron which crushes, it shall break and crush all these. In Daniel chapter 7:7 & 23 it states, "after this I saw in the night visions, and behold, a fourth beast, dreadful and terrible, exceedingly strong. And it had great iron teeth, it devoured and crushed and trampled what was left with its feet. And it was different from all the beasts that came before it, and its ten horns symbolizing ten kings. Thus he said, the fourth beast shall be a fourth kingdom of the earth, which shall be different from all other kingdoms, and shall devour the whole earth, trampled it and break it in pieces.

And as you saw the feet and toes, partly of baked clay of the potter and partly of iron, it shall be a divided kingdom, but there shall be in it some of the firmness and strength of iron, just as you saw the iron mixed with miry clay earthen clay. And as the toes of the feet were partly of iron and partly of baked clay of the potter, so the kingdom shall be partly strong and partly brittle and broken. And you saw the iron mixed with miry clay so they shall mingle themselves in the seed of men in marriage bonds, but they will not hold together for two such elements or ideologies can never harmonize, even as iron does not mingle itself with clay. And in the days of these final ten kings shall the God of heaven set up a kingdom which shall never be destroyed, or shall its sovereignty be left to another people, but it shall break and crush and consume all these kingdoms and it shall stand forever.

Daniel 7:14 states, "And there was given the Messiah dominion and glory and kingdom, that all peoples, and nations, and languages should serve Him. His dominion is an everlasting dominion which shall not pass away, His kingdom is one which shall not be destroyed."

The Apostle John said in Revelation 5:1- 10, which states,

> And I saw in the right hand of Him who sat on the throne a scroll written inside and on the back, sealed with seven seals. Then I saw a strong angel proclaiming with a loud voice, who is worthy to open the scroll and to lose its seals? And no one in heaven or on the earth or under the earth was able to open the scroll, or to look at it. So I wept much, because no one was found worthy to open and read the scroll, or to look at it. But one of the elders said to me, do not weep, behold, the Lion of the tribe of Judah, the Root of David, has prevailed to open the scroll and to lose its seven seals. And I looked, and behold, in the midst of the throne and of the four living creatures, in the midst of the elders, stood a Lamb as though it had been slain, and having the seven horns and seven eyes, which the seven spirits of God are sent out into all the earth. Then He came and took the scroll out of the right hand of Him who sat on the throne. Now when He had taken the scroll, the four living creatures

and the twenty-four elders fell down before the Lamb, each having a harp, and golden bowls full of incense, which are the prayers of the saints. And they sang a new song saying, you are worthy to take the scroll, and to open its seals, for you were slain, and redeemed us to God by Your blood out of every tribe and tongue and people and nation, and have made us kings and priests to our God, and we shall reign on the earth.

In the book Daniel chapter 9:24-27, the Bible says,

> Seventy weeks are determined upon thy people and upon thy Holy city, 490 years to finish the transgression, and to make an end of sins, and to make reconciliation for iniquity, and to bring in everlasting righteousness, and to seal up the vision and prophecy, and to anoint the Most Holy. Know therefore and understand that from the going forth of the commandment to restore and to build Jerusalem unto the messiah there off, shall be seven weeks of years or 49 weeks of years. The streets shall be built again, and the wall, even in troubled times. After three score and two weeks shall the Messiah be cut off but not for himself; and the people of the Prince that shall come shall destroy the city and the sanctuary, and the end There of shall be with flood, and unto the end of the war desolation are determined. He shall confirm the covenant with many for one week: and in the midst of the week he shall cause the sacrifice and the oblation to cease, and for over spreading of abominations he shall make it desolate, even until the consummation, and that determined shall be poured upon the desolate. (Daniel 9:24-27, KJV)

There are two main points to be considered in this prophecy.

1. The word translated "week" in Daniel 9:24 is "*Shabua*" in Hebrew meaning, "seven." Step

In Daniel 9:2, it states

> In the first year of his reign I Daniel by books the number of the years; where of the word of the Lord came to Jeremiah the Prophet that he would accomplish seventy years in the desolations of Jerusalem.

In the book of Jeremiah 25:8-12 the Bible says,

> Therefore, thou said the Lord of hosts because; ye have not heard any words. Behold, I will send and take all the families of the north, said the Lord, and Nebuchadnezzar the king of Babylon, my servant, and will bring them against this land, and against the inhabitants thereof, and against all these nations round about, and will utterly destroy them and make astonishment and a hissing and perpetual desolations and it shall come to pass when seventy years are accomplished, that the land of Chaldean and will make it perpetual desolations. (II Kings 24:1-7, Jeremiah 29:1-10, Luke 3:1-23)

> The Scriptures says in the book of Daniel chapter nine, In the year of Darius the son of Ahasuerus, of the lineage of the Medes, who made king over the realm of the Chaldeans in the first year of his reign I Daniel, understood by the books the number of years specified by the word of the Lord through Jeremiah the prophet, that He would accomplish seventy years in the desolations of Jerusalem. Now while Daniel was speaking, praying, and confessing his sin and the sin of

his people Israel, and presenting his supplication before the Lord his God, while he was speaking in prayer, the man Gabriel, came to him in the evening offering, or prayer time to give him insight of the vision and its understanding.

At the beginning of Prophet Daniel's supplications the command went out, and I have come to tell you, for you are greatly beloved, therefore consider the matter, and understand the vision.

The Seventy Weeks or Seventy years of weeks are divided into three main periods.
(a.) Seven weeks of sevens of the rebuilding of Jerusalem.
(b.) Sixty –two weeks of sevens from the completions of Jerusalem to the time Messiah was cut off.
(c.) One seven, the last seven years of this age ending with the Second Advent of Christ

The First Coming of Our Lord Christ Jesus.

Chapter Two

The Calculations of Prophet Daniel's Vision.

Seventy weeks of years are determined for your people and your Holy city 70 weeks of years multiply by 7 = 490 weeks of years to finish the transgression, to make an end of sins, to make conciliation for iniquity, to bring in everlasting righteousness, to seal up vision and prophecy, and to anoint the Most Holy, Seven weeks of years for restore and rebuilding of Jerusalem, until Messiah the Prince would be seven weeks of years and one week is seven days then we will multiply by seven = **49** weeks of years.   And after sixty –two weeks of years the Messiah shall be cut off, but not for Himself, sixty-two weeks of years multiply by seven = **434 weeks of years.**
Daniel 70th week was **490** weeks of year, Rebuild and restore of Jerusalem 49 weeks of years = **441**
Antichrist shall confirm a covenant with many for one week, One week of year is = 1 week multiply by 7 days of week 7years (441- 434 = 7years)

The tribulation years after the rapture of the Church would be seven years (7), from the time, the Messiah was cut off till the time the Church will rapture is called the period of Grace, God has stopped the watch from the time Jesus died till the time the Church is rapture, and that seven years which is one week of years in Daniel's vision will start to work when believers raptured in heaven, and all those who failed the rapture will pass through hard times that is tribulation. God will not allowed the Church to pass through the tribulation, until the Church is raptured the Antichrist will not come, but after the rapture of the Church then the Antichrist will take control of this world, and those who fail the rapture will pass through seven years of tribulation, the lesser tribulation which is three and half years, and the greater tribulation which is also three and half years will also follows likewise. People of God let us get ourselves prepared for the second coming of our Lord Jesus Christ, for it will happen suddenly, the day and the time no man knows it.

THE TEN KINGS ARE NOT BARBAROUS TRIBES.
And the ten horns out of this kingdom are ten kings that shall arise, and another shall rise after them, and he shall be diverse from the first, and he shall subdue three kings."—Daniel 7:24

Some school of thought teaches that the ten toes and the ten horns of Prophet Daniel's book, chapter two and seven are the ten barbarous tribes which overran the Old Roman Empire between 351-474 A.D. They interpret the little horn of Daniel chapter seven and eight and the beast of Revelation 13-20 to be the papacy, but the following points disapprove this.
1.   The ten toes and the ten horns are explained by God to be ten kings, which have received no kingdom as yet, but receive power as kings one hour with the beast, these shall make war on the Lamb, and these shall hate the whore and shall make her desolate. For God hath put in their hearts to fulfill his will, and to agree, and give their kingdom unto the beast, until the words of God shall be fulfilled (Revelation17:8-17). They are ten persons who will rule ten kingdoms for forty and two months or the last 1260 days at the end of this age, and who will help the beast fight against Christ at Armageddon not ten tribe of the fourth and fifth centuries after the death of Christ.
2.   The ten kings will reign over ten kingdoms that will yet be formed inside the old Roman Empire not ten tribes of the past. Daniel 2:44 and Daniel 7:24.
3.   The God of heaven is to set up a kingdom on earth in the days of these kings.   Daniel 2:44-45 And in the days of

these kings shall the God of heaven set up a kingdom, which shall not be destroyed, and the kingdom shall not be left to other people, but it shall break in pieces and consume all these kingdoms, and it shall stand for ever.

Forasmuch as thou saw that the stone was cut out of the mountain without hands, and that it brake in pieces the iron, the brass, the clay, the silver, and the gold, the Great God hath made known to the king what shall come hereafter, and the dream is certain, and the interpretation thereof sure. He did not set up such a kingdom in 351-474 A.D. and has not yet done so.

4. The ten kings will be in existence at the same time and place, do the same things and continue the same length of time. They will be in existence and be reigning over ten kingdoms before the beast comes. They will make the seventh of the seventh kingdom that precede the beast who forms the eight kingdom. Revelation 17:8-11 The beast that you saw was, and is not, shall ascend out of the bottomless pit, and go on earth shall wonder, whose names were not written in the book of life from the foundation of the world, when they behold the beast that was, and is not, and yet is. And here is the mind which hath wisdom. The seven heads are the seven mountains, on which the woman sitteth. And there are seven kings, five are fallen, and one is and the other is not yet come, and when he comes, he must continue a short space. And the beast that was, and is not, even he is the eighth, and is of the seven, and goes into perdition.

5. The little horn in Daniel chapter seven and eight is the same as the beast in Revelation chapter 13 can be seen by comparison of them in these scriptures, the little horn, since the little horn of Daniel and the beast of the Revelation are the same and are yet future, as proved by their war on Christ at the second advent of Christ, and since they both will have the kings under them at that time, the ten kings could not be ten tribes of the past.

6. Not one detail of Daniel or Revelation has ever been fulfilled with the papacy or ten barbarous tribe outside the empire that overran the Roman Empire centuries ago, tribes could never be ten personal kings as to require of the prophecies of these books. No ten tribes did exist at the same time and place, making agreement to give the papacy the power to rule for three and half years, God did not set up His kingdom in 371- 474 A.D.

7. There were twenty one tribes or more which overran the Roman Empire and not ten, according to the Encyclopedia Britannica any of these group could not exist together to fight against Christ at Armageddon as require in (Revelation 17:14) These shall make war with the Lamb, and the Lamb shall overcome them, for He is the Lord of lords, and the King of kings, and they that are with Him are called, and chosen, and faithful.

8. The papacy did not overthrow three of these tribes and force the others to submit, as predicted of the little horns and the beast. (Revelation 17:12-17, as compared to Daniel 7:8, 19-24) The ten horns which you saw are ten kings who have received no kingdom as yet, but they receive authority for one hour as kings with the beast. These are of one mind, and they will give their power and authority to the beast. These will make wars with the Lamb, and the Lamb will overcome them, for He is Lord of lords and King of kings, and those who were with Him are called, chosen, and faithful.

9. No ten kings have ever come from inside Roman Empire to fulfill the prophecies, as require in Daniel 7:24, Out of this kingdom means from within, the tribe that overran the Roman Empire were from outside that empire.

10. No ten tribes ever been of one mind to give their power to papacy

11. No papacy has ever come from one of the four divisions of the old Grecian Empire as will be true of the little horn of the future, as seen in Daniel 8:9-14, 23

12. No papacy has made constant war on behalf of the saints as the little horn will do when he comes, until Christ the Messiah comes.(Daniel 7:19-22, Revelation 13:1-7,16, 18)

We can, therefore, say without reservation that the theory that the ten kings are ten tribes that overran the Roman Empire 351-474 A.D. is un-biblical and unhistorical. The score of pages in some books devoted to the history of papacy do not prove anything as far as the fulfillment of Daniel's Revelation are concerned, for these events will be fulfilled after the rapture of Churches as proved in Revelation chapter 4:1 After this I looked, and behold, a door was opened in heaven, and at the first voice which I heard was as it were of a trumpet talking with me, which said, Come up here, and I will show you things which must be hereafter. Immediately I was in the Spirit, and behold a throne set in heaven, and one sat on the throne. And He who sat there was, like a jasper and a sardius stone in appearance, and there was a rainbow around the throne, in appearance like emerald.

Luke 3:1-24 states,

> In the fifteenth year of the reign, of Tiberius Caesar, Pontius Pilate is governor of Judea; Herod being tetrarch of Galilee, his brother Philip tetrarch of Ituraea and the region of Trachonitis and Lysanians tetrarch of Abilene. While Anna's and Caiaphas were high priests, the word of God came to John the son of Zacharias' in the wilderness. He went into the regions around the Jordan, preaching a baptism of repentance for the remission of sins, as to be written in the book of the words of Isaiah the prophet saying: The voice of one crying in the wilderness, prepare the way of the Lord, make his paths straight. Every valley shall be filled and every mountain and hill brought low. The crooked places shall be made straight and the rough ways smooth, and all flesh shall

see the salvation of God. Then he said to the multitudes that came out to be baptized by him, Brood of Vipers who warned you to flee from the wrath to come? Therefore bear fruits worthy of repentance, and do not begin to say to yourselves, we have Abraham as our fathers. For I say to you that God is able to rise up children to Abraham from these stones. Even now the axe is laid to the root of the trees. Therefore every tree which does not bear good fruit is cut down and thrown into the fire. So the people asked him, saying what shall we do then? He answered and said to them, "He who has two tunics, let him give to him who has none, and he who has food, let him do likewise." Then the tax collectors also came to be baptized, and he said to them, "Collect no more than what is appointed for you." Likewise the soldiers asked him saying, "What shall we do?" So he said to them, "Do not intimidate anyone or accuse falsely, and be content with your wages." Now as the people were in expectation, and all reasoned in their hearts about John, whether he was the Christ or not, John answered," I indeed baptize you with water, but one mightier than I is coming whose sandal strap I am not worthy to loose. He will baptize you with Holy Spirit and fire. His winnowing fan is in his hands, and he will thoroughly clean out his threshing floor, and gather the wheat into his barn but, the chaff he will burn with unquenchable fire." And with many other exhortations he preached to the people. But Herod the tetrarch, being rebuked by him concerning Herodias, his Brother Philip's wife, and for all the evils which Herod had done, also added this, above all that; he shut John in prison. When all the people where baptized, it came to pass that Jesus also was baptized, and while he prayed, the heaven was opened, and the Holy Spirit descended in bodily form like a dove upon him, and a voice came from heaven said. "You are my beloved Son; in you I am well pleased." Jesus himself began his ministry at about thirty years of age, being as was supposed the son of Joseph the son of Hali.

Was this prophecy fulfilled in the life of Christ? Luke 3:1

Jesus cleanses the Temple: (John 2:13-25)
> Now the Passover of the Jews was at hand, and Jesus went to Jerusalem. He found in the temple those who sold oxen, sheep and doves, and the money changers doing business. When he had made a whip of cords, he drove them all out of the temple with the sheep and the oxen, and poured out the changers money and overturned the tables. He said to those sold doves, take these things away. Do not make my father's house a house of merchandise? Then his disciples remembered that it was written, Zeal for your house has eaten me up so the Jews answered and asked, "What sign do you show us, you do these things?" Jesus answered and said to them, "Destroy the temple, and in three days I will raise it up." The Jews responded, "It has taken forty-six years to build this temple, and you will raise this temple in three days?" But he was talking of the temple of his body. Therefore when he rose from the dead, his disciples remembered that he said to them, and they believed the scriptures and the words which Jesus had said.

In John 6:4- 14it states,

> Now the Passover, a feast of the Jews, was near. Then Jesus lifted up his eyes, and seeing a great multitude coming toward him, he said to Philip, "where shall we buy bread, that these may eat?" But this he said to test

him, for he himself knew what he will do. Philip answered him, two hundred denarii worth of bread is no sufficient for them that every one of them may have a little. One of his disciples, Andrews, Simons Peter's brother, said to him, there is a lad here who has five barley loaves and two fishers, but what are they among so many? Then Jesus said make the people sit down. Now there was much grass in the place. So the men sat down, in number about five thousand. And Jesus took the leaves, and when he had given thanks he distributed them to the disciples, and the disciples to those sitting down, and likewise the fish, as much as they wanted. So when they were filled, he said to his disciples, gather up the fragments that remain, so that nothing is lost. Therefore they gathered them up, and filled twelve baskets with the fragments of the five barley loaves which were le over by those who had eaten. Then those men, when they had seen the sign that Jesus did, said, this is truly the prophet who is Come into the world. Many of the Old Testament prophets prophesied about his birth, his sufferings, his death, burial and his resurrection from the death, and all these had been fulfilled.

Jesus Christ is the Messiah, the savior of the whole world as can be seen in Isaiah 9:6-7 which states, "For unto us a child born, unto us a son is given and the government shall be upon his shoulder and his name shall be called Wonderful, counselor, the Mighty God, The Everlasting Father, of the increase of his Government and peace there shall be no end, upon the throne of David and upon his Kingdom, to order it and to establish it with Judgments and with justice from henceforth even forever the zeal of the Lord of Host will perform.

Chapter Three

The Interpretations on the Second Coming of Christ.

In Acts 4:12, the scripture states, "And there is salvation in no one else, for there is no other name under heaven given among men by which we must be saved." But the name which save lives is Jesus Christ of Nazareth the Savior and the deliverer of the whole world. It is written in the Bible in Matthew 11:28 that, "Come to me all who labor and are heavy laden, and I will give you rest". Jesus Christ is calling all who are having problems, carrying heavy loads who could not bear to come unto him because he has overcome the devil and his demons. Right on the cross of Calvary he gave the devil a technical knockout and he did not raise up his head again.

In another place of the Bible it is written, "The eleven disciples went to Galilee, to the mountain which Jesus directed them and when they saw him they worshipped him but some doubted. Jesus came and said to them, "All authority in heaven and on earth has been given to me." (Matthew 28: 16-18). If all powers belong to Jesus why are you going to the false prophets and idols - witch doctors, come to Jesus and he will deliver you from the hands of the wicked one. In Psalm 1, the bible says, "Blessed is the man who walks not in the counsel of the wicked, nor stand in the way of sinners, nor sits in the seat of the scoffers; but his delight is in the law of the Lord and his law he meditates day and nights. He is like a tree planted by streams of water, that yields it fruits in its season and its leaf does not wither in all that it does he prospers. The wicked are not so but are like chaff which the wind drives away." When one walks with God in all his/her ways, such a person will be blessed by

Almighty God in everything he or she does and he or she will be like a water garden, like a tree besides a river, the tree will be fruitful in season, and the leaves will not wither but always green leaves, that is life of a believer. But the wicked, unbeliever's life is like chaff which the wind blows here and there till he perishes. It is written in another place that the wicked shall depart to Shell (Hell) all the nations that forget God." Don't you know that you have forsaken God to serve another god? So God will count you among the wicked souls whom he will destroy in hell fire.

The first commandment, thou shall have no other gods to worship them. His name is Jehovah but he will become jealous to you when you start to give his glory to idol.

Chapter Four

What Is The Cross And Why Did He Died On The Cross?

Over the years, the cross has been subjected to various uses by different people. The old cartage and Roman Empire used it as a punitive measure. Later, some groups of the occult sciences started using it magically, either to protect or to curse, as well as to conjure evil spirits. Long after Christ's death, some Christians were misled into using it as a protective religious relic. Some people are crazy about using the cross because they believe that their soul's protection is in it. In all these, various people have over looked, misinterpreted or under played the main spiritual significant of the cross. The danger here is that these people knowingly or unknowingly, will their souls to the devil because of the supposed protection or other uses of devilish powers. The Ross is therefore, a compassionate attempt to open people's eyes to the actual spiritual significance of the cross, the dangers in using it the way they do and the way out for those who are already victims of its misuses.

WHAT IS CROSS?

The word cross has a lot of meanings, but for the purpose of the discussion in this book, I will define it according to Oxford Advanced Learners Dictionary, as a stake or post with another piece of wood across it like T, t or X as used in ancient times for "crucifixion." There were different types of crosses use in those days specifically; however, I will discuss about four popular ones. The first one is the simple cross, which in Greek language, is called, "Crux Simplex" –Crux is the

Greek word for cross. This type of cross is just a single board in straight line form

1. Usually, when they used it for crucifying people, they put seats for them; then they would tie the hands up, while the legs were nailed. Many people died on this type of cross.

The second one is usually known as the St. Anthony cross also known as "Crux Commissar" in Greek linage. It is in the form of Capital "T." The third one which looks like a railway crossing "is known as "Crux Decussata" in Greek Language. It means a place where nerves join, form X shape. The final one is the type on which Jesus was crucified. It is a piece of wood like a straight line with another straight piece of wood crossing over the first like small letter "t." the cross is called Crux Imrnissa or the Italian cross. These are the various kinds of crosses, but some of them have been modified, like the Red Cross that has all arms being of equal sizes.

THE TYPES OF CROSS
(1) Crux Simplex
(2) Crux Commissar
(3) Crux Decussata
Sent for the victim
Crux Ansata or ANKH
(4) Crux Immissa or Italian Cross, the type of Cross on which our Lord Jesus Christ was crucified.

WHAT DO VARIOUS PEOPLE USE CROSSES FOR?
Many people are ignorant of what the cross stands for. Often times, many see it as a source of protection, without knowing that each type has what it stands for. Some have evil connotation but so many people that wear them do not know about these dangers.

Times for "crucifixion." There were different types of crosses use those days specifically; however, I will discuss about four popular ones. The first one is the simple cross, which in Greek language, is called, "Crux Simplex" –Crux is the Greek word for cross. This type of cross is just a single board in straight-line form.

THE OCCULTIST USE OF THE CROSS

1. THE OCCULTIST USE: In some churches, people are given crosses to wear on their waist, arms, neck, etc. and people do often wear them as protection. The St. Anthony's cross, for instance, if a small hole is put on it, where one can tie a thread to it, it gives it a completely different meaning "T." The name now changes from crux commissar to crux Ansata, and the witches make use of it. For the witches the Crux Ansata is changed to what they call the Ankh.

2. This they do by putting a curse or blessing on the Crux Ansata and wearing it on the neck all the time. They use the "ANKH" as a form of protection believing that as far as you keep wearing it you will remain protected by them (witches). Some who are aware of these things hide their own crosses, while the ignorant ones just wear them, believing that they are only putting on crosses. The danger however in wearing especially the supposed blessed crosses which many go after, is that one cannot go to the devil for protection without willing his/her soul to him. This is because the supposed blessed crosses are based on devilish powers. Some people are so crazy about wearing these crosses that you dare not touch them or remove them from their crosses, neither dare you touch or remove them from their necks. If you do so they will almost faint because they believe that their sole life protection is in those crosses. Others who have left the substance to pursue the

shadows use them thinking that they are religious relics, but not knowing that they are bonding themselves to the devil.

The occultist and spiritual exorcists have also been using the crosses as a means of exorcism. The esoteric argue that these were in use before Jesus Christ came.

The demoniac usually react violently in the presence of crucifix not necessarily due to Jesus cross. That sounds logical, but reviewing the New Testament accounts, we could see that the presence of Jesus Himself made demons to tremble (Mark 5:6-13). Jesus said behold I give you power to tread upon Serpents and Scorpions, and all the power of the enemy and nothing shall by any mean you. Also after the death of Jesus Christ his disciples equally had power over demons (Mark 16: 17) to cast them out without using a cross but the name of Jesus. The crucifix is not a sacrifice quinoa in the Christian Ministry of deliverance. In fact, it is unnecessary. It is not founded in the Bible. Hence, it is unbiblical. The power to deliver is in the name of Jesus. If you do not have faith in that name as in (John 1: 12), you cannot use it. Remember the story of the seven sons of Sceva in Acts 19: 13-17 who was exorcist but not born again. In fact, the disciples did not use crucifix in deliverance. They only spoke the word and demons obeyed them. The crucifix is unnecessary, since exorcists who are not Christian uses it. It is a kind of white magic. Therefore, do not be carried away by the crucifix as in efficacious religious relics.

11. **PUNITIVE USE:** From the early times up till the time of the early church, the cross was used for capital punishment to crucify those who did abominable things like shooting of armed robbers and other leaders. It was, therefore a way of killing people who were supposed to be completely criminals in the society. In those days, as far back as the era of Carthaginian and

Phoenician wars people were using the cross to punish the offenders. In the Bible as in the Old Testament, it was part of God's law, as recovered in Deuteronomy 21:22-23. "And if a man has committed a sin worthy of death, and he is put to death, and thou hang him on a tree: His body shall not remain all night upon the tree, but thou shall in anywise bury him that day; (for he that is hanged is accused of God). So those who did sacrilegious things in the society and were regarded as abominable persons were sentenced to death by hanging on a tree. They were thereafter buried the same day in one grave, irrespective of their number. Even nowadays when armed robbers are shot, they are carried in boxes and turned over together into a common grave as it was in those days. According to the book of Deuteronomy, any one that hanged on a tree was accused of God. That was the same kind of death that Christ died. That is why Galatians 3:13 says, "Christ hath redeemed us from the curse of the Law, been made a curse for us: For it is written, 'Cursed is everyone that hanged on a tree.' In those days, anyone who died that way were most miserable, because it will be the talk of the town. These people, who were mentioned earlier believe that the cross is used as a form of punishment I for people who have been holy or who speak boldly against the ills of a society since the society would not like them, they kill them by crucifixion. According to them such Holy men may be members of the opposition party to the government in power who were saying something's they felt were not good about the government. The government in order to silence them, would sentence them to death by crucifixion. The heads of the various religious groups are numbered among this group by the esoteric people and they are call the great men that are supposed to be holy actors e.g. Krishna, Hindu, Buddha, Islam, etc. regard these heads all as holy men.

The esoteric people believe in the unification or religions all over the world, saying that all are serving the same God through different ways. So, when Christians regard the death of the Lord Jesus Christ on the cross as being unique the esoteric argue those thousand years before the advent of Christianity, people have been dying on the cross. To them, therefore, the cross does not mean anything or have any unique use than what has been. But from the Scriptures and the facts of history, we will find out whether the death of Jesus Christ on the cross is different from the others.

Chapter Five

The Cross and the Christians.

After the Phoenicians, the Carthaginians also used the cross. The Roman Empire began to use it for the same purpose of destroying people who transgressed their laws. It was during the time that Jesus was crucified. They use it so much that even after Jesus Christ, they crucified upside down. So, it was a 'symbol of shame to the whole world. But the Bible says that, "to us who have been saved, it is the power of God" (See 1 Corinthians 1). It remained a symbol of shame to the world until 312 AD of our Lord Jesus Christ, when Emperor Constantine, one of those who seriously persecuted Christians, had to fight a battle with Maxentius, a skilled soldier who was vast in occlusive powers as well. The two were fighting over Rome. At the last battle, over a bridge, (Bridge of Melvin) that would get Maxentius into Rome, Constantine realized that by military skill and demonic powers he was no match for Maxentius so he prayed to what he called Most High top see him through. Suddenly, because he was worshipping the sun god when the cross appeared over the sun with the words "conquer by this." And that night also in a vision, Christ told him to put that sign (Chi Rho T). The initials of the letter of the name of Christ) on his country's flag. He obeyed and when he went to battle next day, he conquered and entered into Rome. This made him turn from worshiping the sun god to Christianity. The whole Roman Empire was turned to Christianity and the cross became a symbol of victory to them.

Spiritually, the cross is a symbol of victory. It became a spiritual significance on the day Jesus died on it. The day you shall eat of this tree you shall surely die spiritually and finally, he died physically. Death therefore, came over man throughout the generations between thee man and the woman.

And between thy seed and her seed; He shall bruise thy head and thou shalt bruised his heel. That means God after he has punished man with death, quickly promised to send a savior who will save him from spiritual death. It is on'ly the above passage that the phrase "seed of the woman" is used. In another places the Bible uses the seed of the man. In using the former, therefore, the Bible means him incarnation of God into man. That is why we cannot think about the death on the cross without thinking about the incarnation of Christ. Bible tells me that God looked down from heaven to see whether there was any one good. But He found none. No one understood; and consequently, the Lord decided to come and bear the sins of the whole world at the right time. This we, commemorate every year during Easter. From the foregoing, we will find out that His death is not just the death of another "avatar." It was prophesied more than six hundred (600) years before it took place. For instance, David in the psalms prophesied about some of the voiced agonies of the cross. (Psalms 22:1)says, "My God, My God, why hast thou forsaken me?" This is exactly one of the statements of Jesus Christ on the cross as can be seen Matthew 27:46. It may be worthy to point out there that the book of Psalms is not a magic book meant to be put under the pillow and read nineteen times before going to work. It is also not a book to be read in the middle of the night, facing any of the four cardinal points. Any one that uses the psalms in any of these ways is not raising the word of God, but performing occultist rituals. Therefore, be warned so that people don't mislead you into doing any of such things in the name of protection. It is one of the books which the death of Jesus Christ on the cross was prophesized about.

Counting with the Bible Prophesies concerning His death, it was also prophesized that His clothes which He was putting on or wearing was going to be shared and lots cast for it, Psalms 22: 18. They divide his garments among themselves, they crucified Him, and casting lots that it might be fulfilled which was spoken by the prophet. The account of his Death showed that it happened exactly like that Matt. 27:35. Again in Isaiah 53 is almost a complex pre-record of his death. It tells us that Christ came to the world without sin, He counted among the transgressors, Isaiah 53:9. This statement is confirmed in his crucifixion between the two sinners (robbers) Matthew 27: 38. All these prophecies were given more than six hundred-year (600) before he came physically here on this earth. Therefore, he did not just die because he was standing in for the Jews like the other avatars.

Consequently, He was premeditated and purposeful. It was not like god of thunder called Sango who suddenly hanged himself on a tree in Oyo state in Nigeria. It was not like Tweneboa Kodua who said he will die for the Ashanti kingdom, and so they cut his head to be sacrificed for the Ashanti's. I want to assure you that there is only the blood of Jesus Christ, that is worthy which can indeed wipe out our sins and cleanse us to be white as snow. the only perfect sacrifice for the forgiveness of sin. Glory be to God in the highest. Amen! These men both Tweneboa Kodua in Ashanti, Ghana and Sango in Oyo State Nigeria" both of them only committed suicide. Sango in Oyo (Nigeria), it was said he didn't like, What was going on by then but in protest he hanged himself, against the fact that students are being cheated, that person, will have nonstop ticket to hell. Therefore, Jesus death was a big difference, for the fact that God who commanded light to be shine forth with the word of his mouth, came down to take the form of man. He left His glory in Heaven and took flesh of a human being because of his love for man. Isaiah 53:7 says, "He was oppressed, and he was afflicted, yet he opened not His mouth, He is brought as a Lamb to be slaughter and as a sheep before her shavers is dumb, so he opened not his mouth" Hebrews chapter 12:2, "Looking unto Jesus the author and finisher of our faith, who for the joy that was set before him endured the cross, despising the shame, and is set down at the right hand of the throne of God." Jesus handed Himself willingly to be crucified. The people that came to arrest him because, of the power in question. He asked them made all of them fell down twice. That is why Jesus said that, the Son of Man has power to lay down His life and also take it up

People were laughing spitting at Him what He would have done was to shout and millions of angels would come and cleared off all these people. Thank God, however he did not do that, because if he would not have died eventually there would have been no hope for you and I thought the world was created by Him, the world could not recognize Him. Yet decide to humble Himself according to Philippians 2:7-8 "And being found in fashions as a man, he humbled himself and became obedient unto death, even the death on the cross no aviator or religious leader can be compared to what he did neither could they stand him. The Bible says that God therefore has highly exalted Him and give him a name that is above every other name that at the name of Jesus every knee shall bow and every tongue shall confess that Jesus Christ is Lord (Philippians 2:9-11).

THE NATURE OF DEATH

Now, after Pontius Pilate has had Him beaten (flagellum) so seriously that the Bible describes His body as looking like ploughed ground (Isaiah 52:14). The soldiers took him to the cross and nailed Him there on the cross, He was having pity and compassion on His assassins, God by his sufferings was putting our sins on His body that though our sins may die a shameful death on the cross. There at the cross, people kept reviling and mocking Him, "if you are the King of the Jews come down from the cross, so that we will believe you." They said all sorts of things, but He kept quiet. Then by 12 noon the agony was much gain it was when He was praying at Gethsemane. The fact was that it was too much even for a man to behold. An eclipse of the sun then took place so that there was darkness by day. Like the normal eclipse that last not more than five minutes, this one lasted for three hours to show that somebody special. Some argue that it was coincidence. What a wonderful coincidence! He remained in agony, and the Holy Spirit came upon Him so that He began to recite Psalm 22: 1. "My God, My God, why has thou forsaken me?" A little time after, the sun came back and He became thirsty, consequently he request for a drink. They mixed vinegar with some other bitter substances so he couldn't drink it.

MY PRESENCE SHALL GO WITH YOU

And He said, "My presence shall go with you and I will give the rest," Exodus 33:14.
Every human being needs the abiding presence of God. Without it we are truly lonely and constitute an easy prey to the devil, the enemy of our soul. God's abiding presence with a man is worth more than all the monies of the world put together. As a matter of fact, if you have so much money or materials without God at the center of your life you will be frustrated and miserable because real satisfaction will be continually with you. When God is there, there must be joy and gladness, because in his presence is fullness of joy. (Psalm 66:11).

Your provision is adequately guaranteed because he will supply all your needs according to his riches in glory by Christ Jesus (Philippians 4:19). There will be continuous miracles and your life will be a bundle of testimonies because you are constantly enjoying the goodness of the Lord's presence. The presence of the Lord eliminates all fears and brings divinely inspired boldness and confidence. You will fear no man. (Psalm 118:16). You will not be afraid of Satan and the owners of darkness because the great I AM is with you. Your faith is so strong then you are ready for any exploit. If you are so bold in the Lord then you can effectively deal with every crisis. Jesus and his constitute, the unbeatable team but it is the presence of God makes it so real.

No wonder Moses refused to go on when the Lord decided to withdraw His abiding presence from camp of the Israelites (Exodus 33: 1-7). He knew that surely defeat waiting Him if the lord was not there. He told the Lord he was not going to move an inch if His Presence was not going with them.

The Lord went with him, and that was why Moses succeeded the way he did. As you go on with the spiritual warfare insist on and reckon with the abiding presence of the Lord in your life and you shall succeed in every aspect. Although there are hardships and difficulties all around us but when we trust in the Lord, problems will turn to blessings in every way of your life. "You shall increase my greatness and comfort me on every side. (Psalm 71:21). You can confess boldly the scripture that the Lord will increase my greatness and comfort me on every side and so shall it be in Jesus mighty name. In Psalm 37:1-5, it states,

> we have set practical counsels from the Lord on What to do in times like this, to release the promise of the Lord and to enjoy His blessings. Do not fret, whatever may be happening around you reading from yrs. I put your trust in the Lord, He will give you all your heart desires yrs. Delight yourself in the Lord. He will feed you

abundantly years. Commit your ways unto the Lord; He will direct your paths.

Also, Joshua 1:9 states, "have I commanded thee? Be strong and of good courage, he not afraid neither be thou dismayed, for the Lord thy God is with thee wither so ever thy goes". One singular distinguishing mark of the people of God is the divine presence. Wherever God's people are, The Lord is there. In the Old Testament God never left His people. He was with them collectively. He manifested His presence with a pillar of cloud by day and a pillar of fire by night all through the wilderness journey of the Israelites. With the presence of the Lord, no foe was strong enough to defeat them, not even Pharaoh's the greatest military force then on earth. That is to say that the presence of the Lord guarantees complete victory. They were constantly led by the pillar of cloud by day and the pillar of fire by night, divine guidance is assured when the Lord is there. They were miraculously fed with manna from heaven constantly or regularly, even when they desired meat, out of nowhere God provided more than enough for them to eat. The presence of the Lord guarantees abundant provision. The greatest assets the people of Israel had then was been the abiding presence of the Lord (His divine presence). With His divine presence there was nothing their enemy could do to them. That singled them out of all the nations of the world; and Moses reminded them again and again. "For what nations is there so great who has God so high unto them, as the Lord our God is in all the things that we call upon Him for" (Deuteronomy 4:7.)

BETTER COVENANT HERE: Now in the New Testament the issue is raised to another pedestal. God makes abode not just with congregation of believers, but inside every believer. Truly when believers gather together, the Lord Jesus comes to take His throne in their midst to reign in power and Majesty

(See Matt. 18:20). He dwells in our walks and works through us. (2 Corinthians 6:16, Leviticus 26: 11-12.)

The moment you are born again, the kingdom of God comes right in your heart. Christ comes to dwell in your heart by faith through the Holy Spirit (Eph. 3: 17). You become the temple of the living God (Cor. 3:16-17). For every believer it is a privilege to have God with us, this guarantees His abiding presence anytime and anywhere. Therefore, if you have truly given your heart and life to Jesus and you are really born again, you do not need to beg and plead with God to be with you, He is in you already, only by conscious of His presence. Fear thou not; for I am with thee; be not dismayed: for I will uphold thee with my right hand of my righteousness.

VICTORY BY HIS PRESENCE

I would like to summarize what the abiding presence of the Lord will do in your life. "For thou will not leave my soul in hell: neither will thou suffer thy holy one to see corruption. Thou wilt show me the part of life: In thy presence is fullness of Joy; at thy right hand there are pleasures for evermore" (Psalm 16:10-11). It assures that all is well and God is full the Land and denounced what was happening as wrong and evil. When the king inquired is to the source, she out rightly named him: "The adversary and enemy is this vile Haman."(Esther 7:6). Later authorized by King Ahasuerus, Jews rose up and fought against all their enemies, destroying them with the sword and turning the tables (Esther 7:3-5). Instead of shadow boxing we need to properly discern and name evil for what it is and to speak out to authorities about the things that concern us as Christians. We need to directly attack our enemy, Satan, and with our spiritual warfare weapons of praise, prayer, fasting, boldness, faithfulness, through the anointing, the word of God, and love and go on to smash the strong holds of the devil (see Jeremiah 1:10). "See I have this day set thee over the nations and over the

Kingdoms, to root out, and to pull down, and to destroy, and to throw down, to build and to plant. Before one will go to war there must be weapons to fight that war as it is in physical, one can use gun, sword, knife, cutlass, rod, arrow and extra. So it is in the spirit realm, God himself declared that war as it was stated in Genesis 3: 15 and because there is war spiritually there must be provisions of weapons for war against the devil and his demons to destroy all their activities in Jesus powerful name.

CAMPAIGN FOR THE SPIRITUAL WARFARE

Luke 10:17-19 states, "And the seventy returned again with joy, saying, Lord even the devils are subject unto us through thy name. He said unto them I beheld Satan as lighting fall from heaven. Behold I give unto you power to tread on serpents and scorpions and over all the power of the enemy and nothing shall by any means hurt you." You are supposed to make campaign for the battle because Jesus has declared you a winner and Satan the enemy of our soul is already a looser, so be bold and courageous for the war. Warfare means a military Campaign of the Spiritual warfare. We have the weapon that is unity prayer and fasting and the word of God; I encourage you to defend your battle of which God has made you a winner, deem to put down the stronghold of the devil.

THE WICKEDNESS OF HIGH PLACES:

"For the wrestle not against flesh and blood, but against principalities, against powers, against the rulers of the darkness of this world, against spiritual wickedness in 'HIGH PLACES'" (Ephesians 6:12, emphasis added). One of Satan's best kept secrets is the important of the high places in the spirit world. According to the previous bible scripture I came to realize that the devil and his demons rule over nations, towns and villages and the environment. Likewise our churches today because of the ignorance of the ruling Spirit in high place over our cities, must thrill the powers of Israel, warning them about erecting or leaving high places dedicated to idols. "I will destroy your high places, cut down your incense altars and cast your carcasses on the lifeless, from your idols, and my soul shall abhor you. I will lay your cities waste and bring you by establishing these seven basic realities in your spirit day by day, you are preparing to do real spiritual warfare. This is the reason the accuser girths do diligently to rob you of these truths in your life. The accuser knows if you lay these truths represent the basic arteries of your spiritual heart. If you lay these truths in your spirit you will be building the spiritual muscle necessary to destroy his grip on your family, church and nation. This explains why there is such a war for your prayer life. These seven basic truths represent the basic arteries of your spiritual heart. If these arteries got blocked but the accuser, you will have spiritual heart trouble. Notice them carefully. Our father who art in Heaven. Jesus our intercessor declares God as Our Heavenly Father. Jesus paid the price on the cross to bring us back to God. Now, God is our father. This is the very foundation for our spiritual life. If the accuser can keep you from truly knowing God as Father, then your prayers will always be hindered. The Bible says in Psalm 68:5, "A father of the fatherless and a judge of the widows is God in his holy habitation."

Also, the Accuser works by whatever means he can to block the reality of the fatherhood of God from your spirit. Simultaneously, the blood of Jesus is the pure testimony in heaven that cries out "you belong to the heavenly Father." I of a surety bear a child, which am old? Is anything too hard for the Lord? At the appointed time I will return unto thee, according to the time of life, and Sarah shall have a son. Then Sarah denied, saying I laughed not, for she was afraid, and he said nay; but thou didst laugh." Both Abraham and Sarah were advanced in years and there was no hope that they could had a child because Abraham have ceased to be with Sarah after the manner of woman, that proves that they could not meet as husband and wife but when God gives promise he watches over his word to fulfill or to come to pass. In Hebrews 11:11 the Bible says Sarah herself received strength the conceive seed and was delivered a child when she was past age, because she judged him faithful who had promised. Bible tells me about a woman who was called Hannah she was barren, married for so many years but without a child, glory be to God that Hannah prayed and was conceive and gave birth to a child called Samuel. "And they rose up in the morning early, and worshipped before the Lord, and returned, and came to their house to Ramah and Elkanah knew Hannah his wife; and the Lord remembered her. Wherefore it came to pass, when the time was come about after Hannah has conceived that she bare a son, and called his name Samuel saying because I have asked him of the Lord (1 Samuel 1: 19-20).

Also, in Luke Chapter 1:5-7, the bible says, there was in the days of Herod the King of Judea a certain priest named Zachariah of the course of Ahia and his wife was the daughter of Aaron, and her name was called Elizabeth. And they were both righteous before God, walking in all the commandments and ordinances of the Lord blameless. And they had no child, because that Elizabeth was barren, and they both were now well stricken in years. In verse. 24 and after those days his wife Elizabeth conceived, and hid herself five months saying "Thou hath the Lord dealt with me in the days wherein he looked on me, to take away my reproach among men." In Luke 1:37, "For with God nothing shall be impossible." Zachariah was the Priest of God, yet the wife was barren and the Lord Opened her womb and she conceived and bare a son called John the Baptist.

The Almighty God is very powerful to do things. Even when he needs to create something in you that will let you to be productive I believe that he will do it because you have put your trust in him. I know a woman who married for fifteen years no child. Whenever she took in, someone will come and sleep with her in the dream and the pregnancy will be aborted. But when this woman accepted Jesus as Lord and savior we prayed a deliverance prayer for her she conceived and had a son. Sometimes the medical doctors can say that they can't help you, your own situation is hopeless and you cannot have a child. But God who is able to do all things, He said there should be no barrenness in the Land surely God will Fulfill his promise because he is bound by His word. Is there anything, which is hard for God to do? No, for with God all things are possible.

ANNOINTING OIL IN THE PLACE OF DELIVERANCE

Let not thy head lack oil. Oil is very important in the Life of every child of God. Every vehicle needs to change its oil every month so it is in the life of a believing Christian. The anointing will prove your uniqueness, it has the ability to quicken and bring fruits in your life. Anointing will help you to continue and to maintain your destiny. The anointing will bring the balance of the fruits of the spirit as well as the gift of the Holy Spirit. If the anointing is not in your life very soon the enemy will find a way to pull you down. Some people are not looking for the anointing of the Holy Spirit in their lives but they are only finding name (reputation). But your character will place you in position. There are three Kinds of anointing; Individual anointing, believers anointing, corporate anointing. Individual anointing is the kind of anointing which comes on a person to perform a Supernatural work. Believers anointing, is the kind of anointing which come on believers' supernatural enablement to quicken the believer to perform or to do what he can't do with physical strength. Corporate anointing, is the kind of anointing which is very dynamic when a group of people, fellowship, brethren, with one mind praying towards a particular thing, because of the individual anointing that has come together it becomes corporate and it brings immediate results.

The bible says in the books of Isaiah 10:27, "and it shall come to pass in that day, that his burden shall be taken away from off thy neck, and the yoke shall be destroyed because of the anointing. The Almighty God was telling us that a time is coming and this is the time that He will destroy the plans of the very enemy who is fighting against your life.

In chapter 10:38, the Bible says, How God anointed Jesus of Nazareth with the Holy Ghost and with power who went about doing good, and healing all that were oppressed of the devil for God was with him. Jesus could heal sickness and diseases and to set those whom Satan has bound free, because of the anointing. The anointing oil is the symbolic of the Holy Spirit. In James 5: 14, the Bible says is any sick among you? Let him call for the elders of the church and let them pray over him, anointing him with oil in the name of the Lord. And the prayer of faith shall save the sick, and the Lord shall raise him up and if he have committed sins they shall be forgiven him. It has happened in many occasions when we are conducting our deliverance services. People get healed from sickness when we anoint them with oil and prayed for them. Some of them are anointed with oil, yokes started to destroy. Some people are having evil spirit within them, when they are anointed with oil they start manifesting themselves and the evil spirit will eventually cast out from the victim or that person.

Also, in Matthew Chapter 25 from Verses 1-13, we learnt something about the ten virgins. (That is to say ten Christians). These ten, the bible tells us that five were wise when they took their lamp they also took extra oil but the other five were foolish when they took their lamp they forgot to take extra oil. The Bridegroom was delayed so the oil in their lamp got finished, later they heard a voice "Behold the bridegroom cometh" and those were wise put the oil in their vessels, but the fools started to beg. Bible tells us that immediately they came off to buy oil from the sellers the Bridegroom came in and the door was closed. This gives us a clear indication that a Christian without anointing is powerless. Holy Ghost anoints a believer for service. Believer without power or anointing, the devil can trouble such a believer. Let not thy head lack oil, pray to God for power and anointing to destroy the works of the devil that is against your life.

LOOSE HIM AND LET HIM GO

Jesus was resting with His disciples east of Jordan, away from the hostility of the Jews, when word came that His friend Lazarus was sick. Jesus remained two more days then announced to the disciples that Lazarus had died. The disciples, with some reservation followed Jesus back to Bethany, seemingly into the very clutches of the Jewish rulers from whom He had just narrowly escaped. Jesus stopped some distance from Lazarus home where Mary and Martha, his sisters still lived. Jesus sent word privately of his arrival first to Martha, then to Mary. During Jesus discourse with Martha, He told her that her brother will rise again. Martha lapse into her comfortable Jewish theology agreeing with him that Lazarus would indeed rise in the resurrection at the last day, Isaiah 24-25. Martha said unto him, "I know that he shall rise again in the resurrection at the last day."

A tomb is usually a very small place. In fact, many tombs were so small that there was only for one of two bodies. There was a little room of sitting, standing and moving about. Now let's shift our thinking into the spirit realm and examine some spiritual tombs. In other words let's see what spiritual lesson we can learn from the death, burial and resurrection of Lazarus.

Just as there are Laws of nature by which we are bound, such as the law of gravity, the speed of light, and so on, there are also spiritual laws by which we are bound. One of those spiritual laws is found in Romans Chapter 6:23, "the wages of sin is death". In Ezekiel 18:20, the Bible says, "the soul who sins is the one who will die". Since Adam sinned, we have inherited that sin because we are his descendants. That is penalty enough to condemn us to death. In addition to Adam's sin we also have personal sin.

These personal sins are the sins we choose to commit and for which we must eventually collect the wages due that is death. Note that this death is not physical nor is it instantaneous. It is usually drawn out over a long period, often over many years. This slow spiritual occurs, as one becomes a sinful lifestyle one begins to earn the wages connected with it. The cumulative effect of these earned wages builds. For example, the person with his lifestyle lacks any real, lasting, deep contentment. He or she is usually vaguely dissatisfied, feeling empty inside. This dissatisfaction happens even when they are wealthy by the world's standards. Indeed, often the more one acquires, the less satisfaction he or she becomes. Another byproduct of this lifestyle is often a failed or unhappy marriage and a splintered family life. Sadly this person usually ends up surrounding him or herself with people who are just like him, just as self-centered and uncaring as he is.

THE LAW OF FREEDOM

Now there is another law in the scripture, the Law of freedom, found in Galatians 5:1 which states, "Stand fast therefore in the liberty wherewith. Christ hath made us free, and be not entangled again with the yoke of bondage." This verse tells us that one who is born again and who is diligently in the light of the Gospel, standing firm in his or her faith, having clean hands and a pure heart, is the most "free" person in the world. Even if he is in some way physically imprisoned, he is spiritually free. The first man, Adam was certainly free before his fall, wasn't he? God placed him in The Garden of Eden and gave him only one "does not." The only command God made of Adam was that he was not to eat from the tree of knowledge of good and evil. Now I ask you, is that freedom? Adam was free to do anything else he wanted to do. There were no other restrictions; yes that was indeed freedom. Paul also illustrated this principle for us on one occasion he was bound in physical chain; He referred to himself as the prisoner of Christ, Eph. 3: 1. Paul came to know this freedom and he reveled in it.

The only command God gave to Adam was that he ate not from the tree of knowledge of Good and Evil. Now, what do these two spiritual laws teach us? It teaches us that if we live sinful lifestyles we draw a wage that leads to death, which is a spiritual tomb. If we are cleansed by the blood of Christ and choose to live a life of obedience we experience great and wonderful freedom in Christ.

SELF LIFE LEADS TO THE TOMB

Now let's refine this concept of a tomb like lifestyle. Usually when we think of a sinful lifestyle, we think of people committing crime being sexually loose, being addicted to illegal substances, like cocaine Indian herbs, cigarette, drunkenness etc. But there is a Christian Lifestyle that seems innocent of this outward sin yet still leads to the tomb. It is what I call the "self-life". I define "self-life" as a life that is lived for self without any consideration for the will of God or for the good of others. The reason this self-life is so subtle for a Christian is because it doesn't appear evil in itself. It is not listed among the six things the Lord hates (Prov. 16:6) but very real way it leads the Christian into a living tomb as surely as death landed Lazarus there.

How does a Christian end up in the self-lifestyle? It is easy. He gets there by always choosing what is best for him. This person never or only rarely consults or considers the Lord in matters of choice. He just asks, which way is the easiest? Which way gives my flesh gratification? Then he goes with his own answer. Let us look are a very good example in the scripture of self-life and its consequences. In the book of Genesis, Abram (Abraham) and Lot had problems, with each other because of the growth of their respective herds of Cattle. Abraham realized they had to separate so he devised a plan. Now remember, Abram already had God's promise of great blessings for himself and his descendants (Genesis 12:2-3). He believed that word so he knew he could not lose. "So Abram said to Lot, let's not have any quarreling between you and me, or between your herdsmen and mine, for we are brothers. If you go to the left I will go to the right, if you go to the right, I will go to the left. Lot looked up and saw that the whole plain of the Jordan was well watered, like the garden of the Lord, like the land of Egypt, toward Zoar. (This was before the Lord destroyed Sodom and Gomorrah). So Lot's choose for himself the whole plain of the Jordan and set out towards the east. The two men parted company: Abram lived in the land of Canaan, while Lot lived among the cities of the plain and pitched his tent near Sodom. Now the men of Sodom were wicked and were sinning greatly against the Lord (Genesis 13:8-13). Let us analyze this in practical terms. Abraham gave Lot his choice of land and he took what was left. There is no indication that Lot consulted the Lord before he picked. He simply chose the best pasture land, the land that would make his cattle fat, land that would make him rich. Also doing, left the barren, rocky desert land to uncle Abram. But where did it lead him? We all know where Lot's choice led him; he was in Sodom when the Angel of the Lord came to destroyed the City. The angels lets Lot quickly out before destruction of Sodom and Gomorrah.

Again, Lot made a self-life choice. As he was leaving Sodom, the angel told him to flee "to the mountains" but Lot Objected. He asked and received permission to flee "to Zoar."

In John 11:25 – 46, it states,
> Jesus said to unto her, "I am the resurrection, and the life: he that believeth in me, though he was dead, yet shall he live. "Then when Mary came to where Jesus was, and saw him, she fell down at His feet, saying unto him, Lord, if thou had been here my brother had not died. When Jesus therefore saw her weeping, and the Jews also weeping which came with her, he groaned in the spirit, and was troubled, and said where have ye laid him? They said unto him, Lord, come and see. Jesus wept. Then said the Jews, "Behold how he loved him! And some of them said, could not this man, which opened the eyes of the blind, have caused that even this man, which opened the eyes of the blind, have caused that even this man should not have died? Jesus therefore again groaning in himself cometh to the grave. It was a cave, and a stone lay upon it. Jesus said, "Take you away the stone." Martha, the sister of him that was dead, said unto him, Lord, by this time he stinketh for he hath been dead for four days. Jesus said unto her that, if thou believe, thou should see the glory of God?" Then they took away the stone from the place where the dead were laid. And Jesus lifted up his eyes and said, "Father I thank thee that thou hast heard me." And I knew that thou hearest; me always: but because of this people which stand by I said it, that they may believe that thou had sent me. And when he thus has spoken, he cried with a loud voice, "Lazarus come forth." And he that was dead came forth bound hand and foot with grave clothes: and his face was bound about with napkin. Jesus said unto them

loose him and let him go. Then many of the Jews, which came to Mary and had seen the things, which Jesus did, believed in him. But some of them went their ways to the Pharisees, and told them what things Jesus had done.

Lazarus became sick and he died but it was the enemy that caused that death, his death was to glorify the Almighty God. He died and was buried but on the fourth day, when Jesus came the dead man who had no hope was resurrected from death and lived again. Jesus said, "Take away the stone," but Martha said by this time there is a bad odor, Martha indeed was a believer but at that particular time was telling Jesus that there is no hope. It had spoiled and it will be given odor, but Jesus told her that why can't you believe, for with God nothing shall be impossible, if you can believe you would see the glory of God. They took the stone, and Jesus called him to come out from the grave and really he came out, the hopeless man who was given odor became a man of hope because Jesus came in.

The enemy of your life is the devil, who wishes to destroy your life. Put trust in God and seek for deliverance and I believe that Jesus who is the same yesterday, today and forever is still the same. He will set you free from bondage; surely the grave cloths would be no more. Jesus said take it off from him and he was loosed from those problems

The Cross and the Christians.

Chapter Six

What Is The Permanent Resurrection?

Millennial in theological interpretation refers to one thousand-year reign of Christ on the earth. However, there are disagreement as to whether this is an exact figure or an approximate one. Content: There are at least three major schools of theological thoughts on the second coming of Christ.

1. The Amillennialism Position: The Amillennialist believe in the Second Coming of Christ but reject the idea of a millennial reign of Christ on this earth therefore the Amillennialism position which disbelieve Revelation 21 teaches about, the millennial period which is one thousand years reign of Jesus Christ on earth therefore this is said to be false doctrine, for not believing the one thousand years of reign by our Lord Jesus Christ after the Armageddon war.

2. Post Millennial Position: The Premillennialist believe that the world is going to get worse and things will continue to be worse until Christ comes to judge the wicked and sinners and then he will establish his thousand years (1000) reign literally on Earth. The various views of the premillennial position are:

a) Pre-tribulation view: Rapture of the Church will occur before the beginning of the tribulation. This is the one that is true, so many people are confuse with this. The Church will rapture first before the Antichrist will be revealed to take control on this earth. The Holy Spirit is the one who will accompany the Church during the rapture, to meet the Lord in the air before taking us to heaven.

b) Post-Tribulation: Rapture of the church will occur first before the great tribulation come and this is for the Israel as a nation the twelve tribes not the Gentiles.

c) Mid-Tribulation View: Some people also have a view that rapture of the church will occur at the midpoint of the great tribulation. The church will not experience the last half of the tribulation when the suffering will be most severe, but this view is also wrong, the Church will not pass through tribulations, as far as the Holy Spirit is here with the Church, the Antichrist cannot be revealed until the Church is transported to heaven before the tribulations will begin.

Conclusion. Theological interpretations concerning the Second Coming of Jesus Christ are not a point of fellowship among most Christians. All the schools of thought believe that Jesus Christ is coming and that is the most important thing is to believe that Jesus Christ is coming and to get ready or to prepare for the Second Coming of Jesus Christ the Messiah.

THE FIRST RESURRECTION AND THE RAPTURE:

To resurrect means to bring back to use. It simply means revival from disuse, revival from inactivity and it is used to mean bring or come back to life again.

SPIRITUAL RESURRECTION:

Resurrection of the Spirit being quickened from death in trespasses and sins. In Ephesians 4:21-24 the Bible says if so be that ye have heard him, and have been taught by him, as the truth is in Jesus: that ye put off concerning the former conversation the old man which is corrupt according to the deceitful lusts. And be renewed in the spirit of your mind : And that ye put on the new man, which after God is created in righteousness and true holiness. Man was dead when Adam and Eve sinned against God but the gift of God who is Jesus give eternal life.

In Colossians 3: 10, the Apostle Paul writes, "And have put on the new man, which is renewed in knowledge after the image of him that created him. Where there is neither Greek nor Jew, circumcision nor uncircumcision, Barbarian, Scythian bend not free: but Christ is all, and in all. I John 3:9 whosoever is born of God doth not commit sin, for his seed remained in him and he cannot sin because he is born of God. (1John 5:18.)

1 Corinthians 11:7 states, "for a man indeed ought not to cover his head for as much as he is the image and glory of God: but the woman is the glory of the man."

MATERIAL RESURRECTION:

This is the resurrection of the body. It is also called physical resurrection. There are two kinds of material resurrection. These are temporary resurrection and permanent resurrections.

TEMPORARY RESURRECTION:

But when the people were put forth, he went in, and took her by the hand, and the maid arise. The father of this girl came to Jesus and worshipped him, saying, my daughter is even dead, come and lay thy hands upon her and she shall live, through faith Jesus raised the girl up again. In John Chapter 11 the Bible tells me about a certain man whom Jesus loved called Lazarus who died for days but Jesus woke him up. Then Martha said Lord if you were here my brother should not have died. Jesus said I'm the resurrection and life and he that believe in me, though he were dead, yet shall he live: In verse 39 of the same Chapter it states, "Jesus said take away the stone, Martha, the sister of him that was dead, said unto him, Lord by this time he stinketh for he hath been dead four days, And when he thus had spoken he cried with a loud voice Lazarus come forth, and he that was dead come forth".

Also, Luke 7:12-14 states, "Now when he came night to the gate of the city, behold there was a dead man carried out, the only son of his mother she was a widow: and much people of the city was with her. When the Lord saw her, he had compassion on her, and said unto her weep not. He came and touched the bier: and they that bare him stood still. He said, "Young man, I say unto thee arise." He that was dead sat up, and began to speak; he delivered him to his mother. We see again in 1 Kings 17:21-23, "He stretch himself upon the child three times and cried out unto the Lord and said, "Oh Lord my God, I pray thee, let this child's soul come into him, and the child's soul came into him again and he revived. Elijah took the child and brought him down out of the chambers into the house and delivered him unto his mother: and Elijah said, 'See thy son live.'" See II kings 4:34. In Matthew 12:40 Jesus said, "for even as Jonah was three days and three nights in the belly of the sea monster, so will the Son of Man be three days and three nights in the heart of the earth". "But Peter put them all out of the room and knelt down and prayed, then turning to the body he said, Tabitha, get up, And she opened her eyes, when she saw Peter, she raised herself and sat upright(Acts 9:40). It simply means rising up the dead person back to life.

PERMANENT RESURRECTION:

This simply means raised from mortality to immortality to live forever. There are two resurrections in permanent resurrection. These are the first Resurrection and the second resurrection. The first resurrection is the resurrection of the righteous to life before the millennium while the second resurrection is the resurrection of the wicked to damnation after the millennium.

FIRST RESURRECTION:

There are five raptures in the first resurrection. There are:

a) The resurrection of Christ and many Saints that were resurrected after His resurrection. Ephesians 4:8-10 states, "the word of God says wherefore he said, when he ascended up on high, he led captivity captive and gave gifts unto men. Now that he ascended what is it but that he also descended first into the lower parts of the earth? He that descended is the same also that ascended up for above all heavens, that he might fulfill all things."

b) The Bible says in the book of John chapter 14:1-3, "Let not your heart be troubled, you believe in God, believe also in me. In my Father's house are many mansions, if it were not so I would have told you. I go to prepare a place for you. And if I go and prepare a place for you, I will come again, and receive you unto myself, that where I am, there you may be also. Jesus telling us here, there are many mansions in heaven, his Father's house, He promise us that he go to prepare a place for you and I, a time is coming that he will come and take us to his Father's house a place which is prepare for us.

c) God revealed to Apostle Paul, and he said I knew a man in Christ above fourteen years ago, whether in the body, I cannot tell, God knows such an one caught up to the third heaven. And I knew such a man, whether in the body, or out of the body, I cannot tell, God knows. How that he was caught up into paradise, and heard unspeakable words, which it not lawful for man to utter.

d) The rapture of they that are Christ's at His comings for the Lord himself shall descend from heaven with a shout with the voice of the archangel, and with the trump of God and the death in Christ shall rise first: then we which are alive and remain shall be caught up together with them in the clouds to meet the Lord in the air: and so shall we ever be with the Lord. Wherefore comfort one another with another with these words. 1 Thessalonians 4:13-17 But I do not want you to be ignorant, brethren, concerning those who have fallen asleep, lest you sorrow as others who have no hope. For if we believe that Jesus died and rose again, even so God will bring with Him those who slept in Jesus. For this we say to you by the word of the Lord, that we who are alive and remain until the coming of the Lord will by no means precede those who are asleep. For the Lord Himself will descend from heaven with a shout, with the voice of an archangel, and with the trumpet of God. And the dead in Christ will rise first. Then we who are alive and remain shall be caught up together with them in the clouds to meet the Lord in the air. And thus we shall always be with the Lord. This is faithful saying according to God's word that believers will be transfer from this place to heaven to meet Jesus, try to be among of the first resurrection or the rapture of the Saints.

e) The rapture of the 144, 000 Jews saved in the first (3 1/2) three and half years of the tribulation. Revelation 7:1-8 and after these things I saw four angels standing on the four corners of the earth holding the four wind of the earth, that the wind should not blow on the earth or the sea, nor on any tree. I saw another angel ascending from the east, having the seal of the living God: and he cried with a loud voice to the four angels, to whom it was given to hurt the earth and the sea. Saying hurt not the earth, neither the sea, nor the trees till we have sealed the servants of our God in their foreheads. I heard the number of them which were sealed: and there were sealed and hundred and forty and four thousands of all the tribes of the children of Israel of the tribe of Judah were sealed twelve thousands of the tribe of Reuben were sealed twelve thousands of the tribe of Gad were twelve thousand. Of the tribe of Asser were sealed twelve thousand. Of the tribe of Naphtali were sealed twelve thousand. Of the tribe of Manasseh were sealed twelve thousands of the tribe of Simeon were sealed twelve thousand. Of the tribe of Levi were sealed twelve thousand. Of the tribe of Issachar were sealed twelve thousand. Of the tribe of Zebulon were sealed twelve thousand. Of the tribe of Benjamin were sealed twelve thousand. These are the twelve thousand tribes which were sealed, that will be 144, 000 people who will be sealed in all Israel.

f) The rapture of the great multitude of the tribulation saints who will be saved after the rapture of everyone in Christ, whether dead or alive Revelation 7:9. After this I behold, and to a great multitude which no man could number, of all nations, and kindred's, and people, and tongues stood before the throne, and before the lamb, clothed with white robes and palms in their hands. Revelation 5:8-10 Now when He had taken the scroll, the four living creatures, and the twenty four elders fell down before the Lamb each having a harp, and golden bowls full of incense, which are the prayers of the saints. And they sang a new song, saying; You are worthy to take the scroll, And open its seals; For You were slain, And have redeemed us to God by Your blood out of every tribe and tongue and people and nation, And have made us king sand priests to our God; And we shall reign on the earth 1 Corinthians 3:14 If anyone's work which he has built on it endures, he will receive a reward.

Romans 11:25 For I not desire, brethren, that you should be ignorant of the mystery, lest you should be wise in your own opinion that blindness in part has happened to Israel until the fullness of the Gentiles has come in.

g) The rapture of the two witnesses. When they shall have finished their testimony the beast that descended out of the bottomless pit shall make war against them, and shall overcome them, and kill them; their dead bodies shall lie in the streets of the great city, which spiritually is called Sodom and Egypt, where also our Lord was crucified. They of the people and kindred and tongue and nations shall see their dead bodies three days and half, and shall suffer their dead bodies to be put in graves. They shall dwell upon the earth shall rejoice over them, and merry, and shall send gifts one to another: because these two people tormented them that dwell on the earth. Revelation 11:3-4 After three days and half the spirit of life from God entered into them, and they stood upon their feet; and great fear fell upon them which saw them. And they heard a great voice from heaven saying unto them, come up hither. And they ascended up to (heaven) saying unto them, come up hither. And they ascended up to heaven in a cloud: and their enemies beheld them. (Zechariah 4:2-4) And said to me, what do you see? So I said, I am looking, and there is a lampstand of solid gold with a bowl on top of it, and on the stand seven lamps with seven pipes to the seven lamps. Two olive trees are by it, one at the right of the bowl and the other at its left. So I answered and spoke to the angel who talked with me, saying, what are these, my lord? Then I answered and said to him, what are these two olives trees at the right of the lampstand and at its left

The rapture is a spiritual term used to denote the transformation of those in Christ and translation to heaven when the trumpet shall sound.

Chapter Seven

What Are The Qualifications Of Rapture?

SALVATION: One must be genuinely converted or born again. Matthew chapter 18:13 the Word of God says, "And if so be that he find it verily I say unto you, he rejoice more of that sheep, than of the ninety and nine which went not astray. When someone repented from sin the angels in heaven rejoice. Repent ye therefore, and be converted, that your sins may be blotted out, when the times of refreshing shall come from the presence of the Lord."

Jesus answered and said unto him except a man be born again, he cannot see the kingdom of God. Therefore, if any man be in Christ, he is a new creation: old things are passed away, behold, all things are become new. To illustrate this very well when you put a nail near a steam the two will just come together. But as many as received him, to them gave he the power to become the sons of God, even to them that believe on his name.

PURITY OF HEART AND CONDUCT:

Matthew 5:8 states, "Blessed are the pure in heart; for they shall see God." The second qualification of the rapture is to live purified life, without that one cannot see God. Follow peace with all men, and holiness without which, no man shall see the lord. Now unto everyone who is preparing to be with God during the rapture of the church must stay peacefully with men and at the same time live a life of holiness. A life that is challenged or a Christian life. Only the true believers or purity in heart. Saints will see Him. I peter 1:14-16. As obedient

Children, not fashioning yourselves according to the former lusts in your ignorance: But as he which hath called you in holy, so be ye holy in all manner of conversation; because it is written, be ye holy, for i am holy. The bible says wherefore Jesus also, that he might sanctify the people with His own blood suffered without the gate. The blood of the Lord Jesus Christ sanctify all believers and separate us from sin so that one can do the works of God. This is where by a believer is purified in the heart by the Lord, he is cleansed and oiled so as to run away from the Adamic nature from doing evil, bad attitude, evil speaking, wrong communication, backbiting, busy body, and all kinds of evil that can defile man, to turn from them completely unto God wholeheartedly.

SUPREME LOVE FOR GOD:
Philippians 3:7&11 also states,

> But what things were gain to me, those I counted loss for Christ. Yeah doubtless and I count all things but loss for the excellency of the knowledge of Christ Jesus my lord: for whom I have suffered the loss of all things, and do count them but loss, that I may win Christ. If by any means I might gain attain unto the resurrection of the dead. Impress toward the mark for the prize of the high calling of God in Christ Jesus. Let us therefore, as many as be perfect, be thus minded: and if anything ye be otherwise minded, God shall reveal even this unto you. Nevertheless, where to we have already attained, let us mind the same thing.

Genesis 19:12-17 states,
> And the men said unto Lot, hast though here any besides? son in law, thy daughters, and whatsoever thou hast in the city, bring them out of this place. For we will

destroy this place because the cry of them is waxen great before the face of the Lord: and the Lord hath sent us to destroy it. And Lot went out, and spoke unto his sons in law, which married his daughter, and said, up get you out of this place, for he seemed as one that mocked unto his sons in law. And when the morning arose, then the angel hastened Lot, saying Arise, take thy wife and thy two daughters, which are here: let you be consumed in the iniquity of the city, And while he lingered the men laid hold upon his hand of his wife and upon the hands of the two daughters and the Lord being merciful unto him and they brought him forth, and set him without the city. And it came to pass when they had brought them forth abroad, that he said escape for thy life, look not behind thee neither stay in all the plain, escape to the mountains, lest thou be consumed. Then the Lord rained upon Sod-om and upon Go-mor-rah brimstone and fire from the Lord out of Heaven. And it came to pass, when God destroyed the Cities of the plain,that God remembered Abraham,and sent Lot out of the midst of the overthrew the Cities in the which Lot dwelt. You can also look at the following scriptures, Revelation 22:12-17, Mk. 13:32-37, 1Corinthians 10:12.

What is the main purpose of the Rapture?

Then we, the living ones who remain (on the earth) shall simultaneously be caught up along with (the resurrected dead) in the clouds to meet the Lord in the air; and so always (through the eternity of the eternities) we shall be with the Lord! (1Thess 4: 17 from Amplified Bible)

a) To receive saints to Him as promised. in John 14:1-3 it states,

Do not let your hearts be troubled (distressed agitated). You believe in God and adhere to and trust in and rely also in me. In my Father's house are many dwelling places (homes). If it were not so, I would have told you; for I am going away to prepare a place for you. And when (if) I go and make ready a place for you, I will come back again and will take you to myself, that where I am you may be also.

Jesus told his people to expect his coming again, his purpose of coming is to take his followers to His Father's house that is in heaven. Jesus is the husband or the Bridegroom and the church is the Bride of Christ now the husbandman is in heaven and preparing a place for the bride or the church. Jesus is going to wed the church when He takes the church to Himself in heaven.

b) To resurrect the dead in Christ from among the wicked. 1 Theses 4:14 state, "For since we believe that Jesus died and rose again, even so God will also bring with Him through Jesus those who have fallen asleep (in death)." Also, the Bible tells us in Philippians 3:11 that, "if by any means I might attain unto the resurrection of the dead". Paul the Apostle wrote this to the church that there is life after death and all who died in Christ will rise up again to life which he wanted us to be a partaker of the resurrection of the dead during His coming again.

c) To take the saints to heaven to live in the New Jerusalem and receive rewards. In 1 Thessalonians 3:13 it states, "To the end He may establish your heart unblameable in holiness before God, even our Father, at the coming of our Lord Jesus Christ with all his saints".

d) To change bodies of saints to immortality (1 Corinthians 15:35-38) also states, "But some men will say, how are the dead rises up? And with what body do they come? Thou fool, that which thou sowest, is not quickened, except it die. And that which thou sowest not that body that shall be, but bare grain, it may chance of wheat, or of some other grain. But God gives it a body as it hath pleased him, and to every seed his own body.

Who will transform and fashion a new, the body of our humiliation to conform to, and be like the body of his glory and majesty, by exerting that power which enables Him even to subject everything to himself . Phil 3:21. Rapture will be imminent without warning.

Chapter Eight

Events in Heaven and Earth That Will Follow Rapture.

Many theologians are of the opinion that two great events in heaven will follow the rapture. These great events are:
1. The judgment seat of Christ.
2. The marriage supper of the Lamb.

The Judgment Seat of Christ: There are seven different judgments mentioned in the scripture these are the judgments:
  (1) Judgment of believers in sins
  (2) Judgment of believers self
  (3) Judgment of Israel
  (4) Judgment of Angels for rebellion against God
  (5) Judgment of the wicked dead
  (6) Judgment of believers works
  (7) Judgment of the Nations

The Judgment of the Believer Sins:

There is a difference between sin and sins, the word sin is a singular verb that is the Adamic nature as can be seen in Romans 3:23 which states, "For all have sinned and come short of the glory of God". While the word sins is a plural verb which refer to sins like adultery, fornication, backbiting, stealing and all fruits of the flesh, concerning believer's sin Christ paid for it on the cross of Calvary.   (Galatians

5:19-21)We see in John 12: 31-32 stating, "Now the Judgment (crisis) of this world is coming and sentence is now being passed on this world. Now the ruler (evil: genius prince) of this world shall be cast out (expelled). And I, if and when I am lifted up from the earth (on the cross), will draw and attract all men (Gentile as well as Jews) to myself." Believers as to sin can be seen in Romans 6:10-11 stating, "for in that he died unto sin once: but in that he lived unto God. Likewise reckon you also yourselves to be dead indeed unto God. Likewise reckon you also yourselves to be dead indeed unto sin, but alive unto God through Jesus Christ our Lord."

Time on the cross Jn. 3:14.
"And as Moses lifted up the serpent in the wilderness, even so must the Son of man be lifted up. That whosoever believeth in Him should not perish, but have eternal life. "

The Judgment of Believers (Self):

Believer's self-judgment is accounting for moral and spiritual conduct daily or self-examination or total consecration. This makes the believers to be Christ conscious which makes him or her to live a holy life. The subject of these judgment are believer walking in the light and the time is every day.

Basis: Obedience to God and His word. James 1:22-26:
Be ye doers of the word, and not hearers only, deceiving ourselves. If any be a hearer of the word, and not a doer, he is like unto a man beholding his natural face in a glass. For he behold himself, and get his way, but who's looked into the perfect law of liberty, and continuity therein he was. But a doer of the work this man shall be blessed in his deed. If any man among you seem to be religious, and bridle not his tongue, but deceive his own heart, this man's religion is in vain.

Pure religion and undefiled before God and the Father is this to visit the fatherless and widows in their affliction, and to keep himself unspotted from the world. All what the Bible is telling us is that Christians who refuse to judge themselves will lose their salvation. 1 John. 1:7 But if we walk in the light as He is in the light, we have fellowship one with another and the blood of Jesus Christ His Son cleanest us from all sin.

The Judgment of Israel: Israel as a nation for many years or centuries of rebellion to God. Ezekiel 20:33-34: "As I live, says the Lord God, surely with a mighty hand, and with a stretched out arm, and with fury poured out will I rule over you. And I will bring you out from the people and will gather you out of the countries where in ye are scattered, with a mighty hand, and with stretched out arm, and with fury poured out."

The Israelites were scattered throughout the whole world and God has promised that he will gather them together again and this prophecy is what is going on today, all the Israelites are going back home and this tells us that God's word is very true. Israel as a nation doesn't believe that their Messiah is Jesus who came, they are still expecting the Messiah. Israel will pass through the small tribulation which is three and half years, which God will select 144, 000 preachers to evangelize the nation of Israel when the small tribulation comes to an end, then Israel will realized that their Messiah is Jesus who came to died and they will cry to him, and the Lord will save them:

Venue: Palestine, Moab, Edom
Basic: obedience to God and word to God
Result: Mass Conversion of Israel during Second Advent: (Isaiah 1:27) Zion shall be redeemed with judgment and her converts with righteousness.

Ezekiel 22: 19-22: "Therefore thus says the Lord God: because ye are all become dross, behold therefore I will gather you into the midst of Jerusalem. As they gather silver, and brass and iron and lead, and tin, into the midst of the furnace, to blow the fire upon it to melt it; so will I gather you in mine anger and in my fury, and I will leave thee and melt you. Yeah, I will gather you, and blow upon you the fire of my wrath and ye shall be melted in the midst thereof. As silver is melted in the midst of the furnace, so shall ye melted in the midst thereof, and ye shall know that I the Lord have poured out my fury upon you.

Judgment of Angels:

The judgment of Angels for rebellion against God can be seen in 2 Peter 2:4 which reads "for if God spared not the angels that sinned, but cast them down to hell, and delivered them into chains of darkness, to be reserved unto judgment." Also, we can see it in Jude 1: 6-7: "and the Angels which kept not their first estate, but left their own habitation, he hath reserved in everlasting chains under darkness unto the judgment of the great day. Even so Sodom and Gomorrah, and the cities about in like manner, giving themselves over to fornication, and going after strange flesh are set forth for example, suffering the vengeance of eternal fire." The judgment of the Angels will be after the millennium, the great white throne judgment. They are the fallen angels (See Revelation 12:7-12). In 1 Corinthians 6:3, the Apostle Paul wrote "know ye not that we shall judge angels? How much more things that pertain to this life? The Judgment of angels will take place in heaven before the great white throne judgment. In Revelations 20:11-15, John writes,

> and I saw the great white throne, and him that sat on it from whose face the earth and the heaven fled away;

and there was found no place for them. And I saw the dead, small and great stand before God, and the books were opened, and another book was opened which is the books of life; and the dead were judge out of these things which were written in the books according to their works and he gave up the dead which were in it and the dead and hell delivered up the dead which were in them: and they were judged every man according to their works. And death and hell were cast into the Lake of fire. This is the second death. And whosoever was not found written in the book of life was cast into the lake of fire.

    The judgment of believer's works: the panel of the judgment will be God the Father, God the Son, and God the Holy Spirit. The Father will decree, and the Son will execute the judgment. Acts 10:42 and he commanded us to preach unto the people, to testify that it is he which was ordained of God to be the judge of quick and dead.

    The judgment will be visible personal trial not just spiritual; it will be a universal judgment. Acts 17:31: "because he hath appointed a day, in which he will judge the world in righteousness by that Man whom He hath ordained: where He has given assurance unto all men, in that He hath raised him from the dead."

The judgment of believer's work is called the Bema judgment. God is not going to judge the sin of the believers but he will judge the works of the believers'. Roman 14:10 But why dost thou judge thy brother? Or why dost thou set at ought thy brother? 2 Cor. 5:10. For we must all appear before judgment seat of Christ; that every one may received the things done in his body, according to that he hath done, whether good or bad. The first thing in one's life is sin and when he or she accepts Christ in his life he becomes son of God, and then God gave certain works to his children this is called stewardship.

   (1) Believers will be judge according to John 3:16-18. (1 Corinthians 3: 13:) "Every man work shall be made manifest: for the day shall declares it because it shall be revealed by fire, and the fire shall try every man work of what sort it is. If any man's work abide which he hath built thereupon, he shall receive a reward. If any man work shall be burns, he shall suffer loss: but he himself shall be saved: Yet so as fire. (Our works will be judge and tested with fire).

   (2) Matthew 15:19-30, Our thought will be judge for out of the heart proceed evil thoughts, murders, Adulteries, fornications, thefts false witness, blasphemies, these are the things which defile a man: but eat with unwashed hands defiled not a man.

   (3) Our words will be Judge Matthew 12:36-37, But I say unto you, that every idle word that you shall speak, they shall give account thereof on the Day of Judgment for thy words thou shalt be justified and by thy words thou shalt be condemned.

   (4) Our secret shall be judge. Romans 2: 16, in the day when God shall judge the secrets of men by Jesus Christ according to my gospel.

   (5) Our motives shall be judge; the correct motives that which contains in the word of God.

     a. Conscience Rom. 8:15 for you did receive the spirit of bondage again to fear, but you received the spirit of adoption by whom we cry out Abba Father. God has placed conscience in the life of every man, sometimes you do something, and your conscience begin to talk to you, don't you know that what you did was wrong, you should have done it this way. Apostle said in his writing that he has a good conscience. Acts 23:1 Then Paul, looking earnestly at the council, said, Men and brethren, I have lived in all good conscience before God until this day.

b. Book of secret works Rom 2: 16 in the day when God will judge the secrets of men by Jesus Christ, according to my gospel. (Ecclesiastes 12:14) For God shall bring every work in judgment, with every secret thing, whether it is good or evil. Acts 17:30-31 truly, these times of ignorance God overlooked, but now commands all men everywhere to repent, because He has appointed a day on which He will judge the world in righteousness by the Man whom He has ordained. He has given assurance of this to all by raising Him from dead. 1 Corinthians 4:5 Therefore judge nothing before the time, until the Lord comes, who will both bring to light the hidden things of darkness and reveal the counsels of the hearts. Then each one's praise will come from God.

c. Book of words Matthew 12:36-37: But I say to you that every idle word men may speak, they will give account of it in the dad of judgment day. For by your words you will be justified, and by your words you will be condemn. We must be watchful about what comes from our mouth, because God will bring it to judgment, every idle words which will proceeds from our mouth, you must be very careful

d. Book of public works Matthew 16:27

e. The Book of Life Revelation 20:15

Judgment of the nations and wicked dead.

The difference between the judgment of nations and wicked dead is that:

1) The judgment of living nations will be on earth while the judgment of the wicked dead will take place in heaven.

2) The judgment of the nations will take place at the beginning of the Millennium while the judgment of wicked dead will be after millennium reign. There will be one thousand years between judgment of nations and the judgment of the wicked dead.

The subject of the judgment of the living nation is the Gentiles alone while the judgment of the wicked to dead will comprise both the Jew and the Gentiles—who will not be saved. The purpose of the judgment of nations is to know those who will be on earth during the millennium while the judgment of wicked to dead is to take them to hell. The judgment of wicked dead these include all wicked men from Adam to the end of Millennium.

THE CROWN OF GLORY

The crown of glory is a reward for the faithful, obedient God called pastor. It is a crown for dedicated chosen shepherds who are ready to lay down their lives for the sheep. This crown is not for those men who suddenly became pastors in order to make a living. The crown is a testimony for every faithful, obedient, and dedicated God-called pastor that their ministry on earth is pleasing and acceptable to Christ, the Chief Shepherd.

> "The Elders which are amongst you I exhort, who am also an elder, and a witness of the sufferings of Christ, and also a partaker of the glory that shall be revealed; feed the flock of God which is among you taking the

oversight thereof, not by constraints but willingly, not for filthy lucre, but of a ready mind neither as being lords over God's heritage, but being examples to the flocks. And when the Chief Shepherd shall appear, ye shall receive a crown of Glory that faded not away. (1 Peter 5:1-4).

The crown of glory is also called the crown of pastors.

THE CROWN OF RIGHTEOUSNESS

A believer is made righteous at the time of conversion. He is made the righteousness of God in Christ, and can claim and stand in this saving righteousness. Saving righteousness is a gift, given to those who are justified by the sacrifice of the Lord Jesus. The crown of righteousness, however, must not be confused with the gift of righteousness. The crown of righteousness is a reward to be earned by the souls who keep the faith, keep the whole counsel of God, preach it and live in it. 2 Timothy 4:7-8: "I have fought a good fight I have finished my course, I have kept the faith. Hence, forth there is laid up for me a crown of righteousness, which the Lord, the righteous judge, shall give me at that day, and not to me only, but unto all them also that love his appearing." Philippians 4:8: "finally, brethren, whatsoever things are true, whatsoever things are honest, whatsoever things are just, whatsoever things that are pure, whatsoever things that are lovely, whatsoever things are good report: If there be any virtue, and if there any praised, think of these things." The name for the crown of righteousness is called crown of Anticipators. Every Christian aspiring for the crown of righteousness must be prepared to sacrifice all and even suffer hard ship for the testimony of Christ. It is a crown for those who are not bothered by the Jeers and Scoffs of men, nor deterred by the Cynicism of the distractors. The crown is for men and women who are strong in intercession and, as such giving birth to generations of children in the Lord through their increasing efforts. This crown is for those who love the appearing of the Lord and patiently working for Him.

2 Corinthians 6:4: "But in all things approving ourselves as the minister of God, in much patience, in afflictions, in necessities, in distress in stripes, in labors in watching, in fasting; By pureness, by knowledge, by longsuffering, by the word of truth, by the power of God, by the amours of righteousness on the right hand and on the left. By honor and dishonor, by evil report and good report; as deceived and yet true, as unknown, and well known as dying and behold, we love, as Chastened, and not killed, as sorrowful yet always rejoicing as poor yet making many rich, as having nothing and yet possession all things.

Whatever situation that may come in the way of a believer we must endeavor to keep the faith, do the work of God ceasing or unceasing period. When the Apostles Paul and Silas were imprisoned they did not kept silence, they knew that because of the truth that they were arrested, they were beaten and chained both legs and hands but when they prayed and sang a song unto the Lord, God Almighty delivered them from the hand of the wicked one. They did what was right in the sight of God which proves to me that God will in turn also reward them with the crown of righteousness, if we suffer for Him, we shall be rewarded with the crown of righteousness.

THE CROWN OF LIFE

James 1:12 states, "blessed is the man that endure temptation for when he is tried, he shall receive that which the Lord hath promised to them that love him." The Bible says for whosoever will save his life will lose it; but whosoever shall lose his life for My sake and the gospel's the same shall save it. The gift of eternal life is received by every believer at salvation, his possession for eternity however, not all Christian will be rewarded with the crown of life. The crown of life is a reward for a believer who loves the Lord. It is for those Christians who are ready to endure trials and temptations daily. There will be treasured reward for men and women who are of high integrity and moral excellence; men and women who are bold and stand for the standards of Christ. The crown for life is for those who have been tried, tested, persecuted and or even martyred for the truth.

THE CROWN OF REJOICING

This is also known as soul winner's crown. Believers who are soul winners will ultimately receive the crown of rejoicing. "Ye have not chosen me, but I have chosen you and ordained you, that you should go and bring forth fruit, and that your fruit should remain; that whatsoever ye shall ask from the Father in My name He may give it to you." John 15:16.
Every tree which bears fruits is very useful for the owners because when it reaches the season of that fruit the owner will gain from it. Let us take for instance Bishop Emmanuel planted cocoa in his farm after three years the cocoa started to bear fruits, because of that Bishop gained much money from these fruits which the cocoa farm bears or produce every season. Bishop Emmanuel will rejoice during cocoa season, the same is like a Christian who win souls he too will rejoice like that cocoa farmer. "For what is our hope, or crown of rejoicing? Are not even ye in the presence of our Lord Jesus Christ at His coming? For ye are our glory and joy." Every soul won to the Lord by the believer will attract a gift of the crown of rejoicing from the Lord to the believer.

The degree of joy that every believer will have in heaven will be determined by the part the believer has played in bringing many souls to Christ Jesus. This reward, however, is not given according to the success of labor, but according to motive and faithfulness in bringing many to Christ. "The fruit of righteousness is a tree of life, and he that wins souls is wise." (Proverbs 11:30)

Those Christians who have never won any souls to Christ will lose this reward. The crown of rejoicing is like a ball of dazzling light. Hence, soul's winners will shine forever, flowing from one part of heaven to the other with an equally beautiful crown to match. Since soul winners will shine as stars forever, we can assume that the number of stars on the crown of rejoicing on each soul winner's head depends on the number of souls won to the Lord (Daniel. 12:3). This is the time that we can do the Lord's business of soul winning to bring the lost souls to Christ by means of telling them about Jesus, our testimonies also is more effective to draw souls to Jesus as well as what He has done for us since He called you to Himself or to His Kingdom. Let us not close our mouth but rather let us open to testify or witness Christ to people and the Lord will confirm His words by means of saving souls through us.

THE CROWN OF INCORRUPTIBLE

This crown is for Christians who present their bodies as living sacrifices, Holy and acceptable unto the Lord as an acceptable service (Romans. 12:1). Aspiring to receive this reward is a competition. It is a race. In this race, the believer does not compete with anyone but with himself/ herself aspiring to observe the rules which are found in the scriptures. The competitor must deny himself of anything that would weigh him down and hold him back (Hebrews 12:1). Since qualification for entering into this spiritual race is found in the new birth, the competitor then must be born again. Every believer who is involved in this race must fix his eyes permanently on Christ and not be distracted by anything else; he or she must obtain strength from the Lord Jesus Christ. Every believer who must be among this competition must sacrifice all other conflicting competitions for the sake of concentrating all on the race.

The flesh must be put in his proper place. It must be handle roughly and brought under the permanent control of the human spirit.

The craving, desires and the passions of the flesh must be tamed see. (1 Corinthians 9:24-27) states,

> Know you not that they which run in a race run all, but one receives the prize? So run, that ye may obtain. And every man that strives for the mastery is temperate in all things. Now they do it to obtain a corruptible crown; but are incorruptible. I therefore so run, 0not as uncertainty, so fight I, not as one that beaten the air, but I keep under my body and bring it into subjection, that lest by means, when I have preached to others I myself should be a cast out.

(2. THE MARRIAGE SUPPER OF THE LAMB

The marriage supper of the Lamb will take place in heaven just before the Second Advent of Christ to the earth. "Let us be glad and rejoice, and give honor to Him: For the marriage of the Lamb is come and his wife hath made herself ready. And to her was granted that she should be arrayed in fine linen, clean and white: for the fine line is the righteousness of the Saints. And he said unto me, write blessed are they which are called unto the marriage supper of the Lamb. And he said unto me, these are the true sayings of God." (Revelation 19:7-9)

The Bridegroom or the husbandman is now in heaven waiting for the bride, who is the church or the wife to finish her preparation. Here on this earth when two couples are getting marry, the man (Bridegroom) will first come to the church while the wife (Bride) will also be at home making preparation to meet his husband at the church for the marriage.

When people see the man in the church it proves that the marriage or the wedding ceremony is surely coming on. Jesus Christ who is the husband of the church is now in heaven, surely this marriage will come on, and it will never fail. This marriage must surely come to pass so brethren endeavor to get prepare toward that to meet Jesus at the wedding ceremony in heaven.

The wife or the bridegroom is the redeemed ones of all ages who will have part in the first resurrection and who will live in the New Jerusalem forever. According to Revelation 21:2, 9-10 the Bible says,

> And I John saw the Holy City New Jerusalem coming down from God out of heaven, prepared as a bride adorned for her husband. And there came unto me one of the seven vials full of seven last plagues and talk with me saying come hither, I will show thee the bride, the Lamb's wife. And he carried me away in the Spirit to a great high mountain, and showed me that great city, the holy city descending out of heavens from God.

The church, the bride and the wife of Christ is now married. The marriage supper of the Lamb is the concluding ceremony of the marriage between the Lamb and the Bride. It is not the marriage contract entered into between Christians at conversion. "If a damsel that is a virgin be betrothed unto a husband, and a man find her in the city, lie with her, then ye shall bring them both out unto the gate of that city and ye shall stone them with stones that they die, the damsel, because she cried not, being in the city, and the man, because he hath humbled his neighbors wife, so thou shall put away evil from among you." (Deuteronomy 22:23-24) "Then Joseph her husband, being a just man, and not willing to make her a public example, was minded to put her away privately   or secretly" (Matthew 1:19). Let marriage be held in honor (esteemed worthy, precious, of great price, and especially dear) in all things. And thus let the marriage bed be undefiled (kept dishonored); for God will judge and punish the unchaste (all guilty of sexual vice and adulterous.)

Events in Heaven and Earth That Will Follow Rapture.

Chapter Nine

Events That Will Take Place between Rapture And Revelation.

Eight events will take place between the rapture and revelation. The first event which will take place will be the presentation of saints before God. The Bible says in Ephesians 5:27 that He might present it to Himself a church, not having spotted or wrinkle, or any such thing: but it should be without blemish. Saints will be settled in Mansions.

According to John 14:1-3, Jesus said, "that let not your heart be troubled: ye believe in God, believe in me also, in My Father's house are many mansions. If it were not so I would have told you. I go to prepare a place for you, I will come again, and receive you unto myself, that where I am, there ye may be also." There shall be a regular worship of God by the saints. Preparation of the Second Advent, the battle of Armageddon, and the establishment of the eternal government on the earth. The marriage supper of the Lamb will be held in heaven (the atmospheric heaven). Some scholars believe that both the judgment seat of Christ and the Marriage Supper of the Lamb will take place in the air after Christ raptures the Saints, other school of scholars however, believe that at the rapture the saints will go immediately to heaven where they will remain during the last seven years of this age and during the tribulation. The word of God tells me in 1 Thessalonians 4: 16-17 that, "for the Lord himself shall descend from heaven with a shout, with the voice of the Archangel, and with the trump of God; and the dead in Christ shall rise first. Then we which are alive and remain shall be caught up together with them in the clouds, to meet the Lord in the air; and so shall we ever be with the Lord."

The Greek word used to denote marriage in Revelation 19:7 is *Gamos* and it simply mean marriage feast. Let us be glad and rejoice and give honor to him, for the marriage of the Lamb is come and his wife hath made herself ready. This translates marriage according to Revelation 21:7-9, "The bible says He that overcome shall inherit all things, and will be his God, and he shall be my son. But the fearful and unbelieving, and the abominable, and murderers and whoremonger and sorcerers and isolators and all liars, shall have their parts in the lack which bummed with fire and brimstone which is the second death. And there came unto me one of the seven angels which has the seven vials full of the seven last plagues, and talked with me, saying come hither, I will show thee the bride and the Lamb's wife." It is also translated wedding Luke 12:36. And ye yourselves like unto men that wait for their Lord, when he will return from the wedding, that when he cometh and knocked, they may open unto him immediately.

The Bride of Christ is not Israel of old Testament time, not a part of the New Testament church, not the whole new testament churches, not the 144,000 Jews, not the tribulation saints, not any single individual or any one special group of individual out of the redeemed. The bride of Christ is not any one demonstration or all denominations combined. The church, bride of Christ, is now married. Christians are married to Christ, the gospel according to Mark 2:19, "and Jesus said unto them, can the children of the bride chamber fast, while the bridegroom is with them? As long as they have the bridegroom with them, they cannot fast, but the days will come, when the bridegroom shall be taken away from them and then shall they fast in those days." Christians are married to God under the terms of the New Testament as Israel was married to God under the terms of the Old Testament. The concluding of festivities, however took place at the actual time coming together as husband and wife, at which time a marriage supper was given. The marriage was consummated by entrance into the wedding chamber. As at present the church is betrothed to Christ and as such, legally (and spiritually) married. The marriage supper of the Lamb in Revelation nineteen then is just concluding ceremony of the wedding but not the same as the marriage contract entered into a conversion (betrothal).

ANTICHRIST

The name Antichrist means against Christ. That is "Antichrists" the spirit of one who opposes Jesus Christ. It also means the one who takes the place of Christ. The bible tells me in 2 Thessalonians 2:4, "that who opposed and exalted himself above all that is called God, or that is worshipped, so that he as God sitteth in the temple of God showing himself that he is God"

NAMES OF ANTICHRIST

(1) The bloody and deceitful man: "Thou shall destroy them that speak leasing the Lord will abhor the bloody and deceitful man" (Psalm 5:6). God is absolutely holy so he cannot take pleasure in wickedness, so the evil one cannot dwell in His presence and cannot tolerate the foolish booster. God hates the workers of iniquity, He hate leasing falsehood. God abhors bloody men and deceitful one.

(2) The wicked one: the wicked in his pride doth persecute the poor: let them be taken in the devices that they, have imagined. For the wicked boasted of his heart's desire and blessed the covetous whom the Lord abhorred. The wicked, through the pride of his countenance will not seek after God. God is not in all his taught Psalm 102:2-4

THE MAN OF THE EARTH

To judge the fatherless and oppressed, that the man of the earth may no more oppress Psalm 10:18. Seven future events predicted.
  (1) "The arm (flower) of the wicked will be broken in the millennium" (Psalm 10:15).
  Then cometh the end when he shall have delivered up the kingdom of God, even the father, when he shall have put down all rule and all authority and power for he must reign till he hath put all enemies under his feet. The last enemy that shall be destroyed is death. For he hath put all things under his feet. But when he said all things are put under him, it is manifest that he accepted which did put all things under him. And when all things shall be subject unto him that put all things under him that God may be all in all. 1 Cor. 15:24-28

THE MIGHTY MAN

"Why boasts thou thyself in mischief, 0 mighty man? The goodness of God endured continually" (Psalm 52:1)

THE ENEMY

"Because of the voice of the enemy, because of the oppression of the wicked: for they cast iniquity upon me, and in wrath they hate me." (Psalm 55:3)

THE ADVERSARY

"They said in their hearts, let us destroy them together: they have burned up all the synagogues of God in the land. We see not our signs: there is no more any prophet: neither is there among us any that know how long. O God, how long shall the adversary reproach shall the enemy blaspheme they name or ever?" (Psalm 78:8-10)

THE VILE PERSON

> And in his place or office (in Syria) shall arise a contemptuous and contemptible person to whom royal majesty and honor of kingdom have not been given. But he shall come in without warning in the time of security and shall obtain the kingdom by flatteries, intrigues, and cunning, hypocritical conduct out of littleness and shall and small beginnings one of them came forth (Antiochus Epiphanies) a horn whose impious presumption and pride grew exceedingly great towards the south and toward the east and toward the ornament (the precious blessed land of Israel. In my vision this horn grew great even against the host of heaven (Gods true people and saints) and some of the host and of the stars (priests) it cast down to the ground and trampled on them.

And at the latter end of their kingdom when) the transgressors the apostate Jews) have reached the fullness of their wicked taxing the limits of God's mercy) a king of fierce countenance and understanding dark trickery and craftiness shall stand up.

THE WILLFUL KING

> "And the king shall do according to his will: he shall exalt himself and magnify himself above every god and shall speak astonishing things against the God of gods and shall prosper till the indignation be accomplished for that which is determined (by God) shall be done. He shall not regard the god of his father's or him (to whom women desire to give birth --

the Messiah or any other God, for he shall magnify himself above all." (Daniel 11:36-37)

THE MAN OF SIN

"For the mystery of lawlessness that hidden principle of rebellion against constituted authority is already at work in the world (but it is) restrained only until he who restrains it is taken out of the way. And then the lawlessness one (the antichrist) will be revealed and the Lord Jesus will slay him with the breath of His mouth and bring him to an end by his appearing at His coming." (2 Thessalonians 2:7-8)

> The coming of the lawless one (the antichrist) is through the activity and working of Satan and will be attended by great powers and with all sorts of (pretended) miracles and signs and delusive marvels all of them) lying wonders. "But with righteousness and justice shall He judge the poor and decide with fairness for the meek, the poor, and the downtrodden of the earth, and He shall smile the earth and the oppressor with the rod of His mouth and with the breath of His lips He shall slay the wicked". (Daniel 11:4)

PERDITION

Let no one deceive or beguile you in any way, for that day will not come except the apostasy comes first (unless the predicted great falling away of those who have professed to be Christians has come and the man of lawlessness (sin) is revealed, who is the son of doom (of perdition). But the Holy Spirit distinctly and expressly declares that in latter times some will run away from the faith, giving attention to deluding and seduction spirits and doctrines that demons teach. And he shall speak against the Most High God and shall wear out the saints of the Most High and think not change the time of the sacred feast shall be given into his hand for a time, two times and half a time (three and half years) But the judgment shall be set by the court of the Most High) and they shall take away his dominion it (suddenly in the end. "As I stood on the sandy beach, I saw a beast coming up out of the sea with ten horns and even heads. On his horns he had ten royal crowns (diadems) and blasphemous title names on his heads. And the beast that I saw resembled a leopard, but his feet were like those of a bear and his mouth was like that of a lion. And to him the dragon gave his (own) mighty and power and his (own) throne and great dominion. And one of his heads seemed to have a deadly wounds. Bit his death stroke was healed and the whole earth went forth after the beast in amazement and admiration.

>They fell down and paid homage to the dragon because he had bestowed on the beast all his dominion and authority and they also praised and worshipped the beast, exclaiming, who is a march for the beast and who can make a war against him. And the beast was given the power of speech uttering boastful and blasphemous word and he was given freedom to exert his authority and to exercise his will during forty two months (three and half years). And he opened his mouth to speak slanders against God, blaspheming, his name and His abode (even verifying) those who live in heaven. He was further permitted to wage was on God's holy people (the saint) and to overcome them. And power was given to him to extend his authority over every tribe and people and tongue nation" (Revelation 13:1-7)

Events That Will Take Place between Rapture And Revelation.

THE LAWLESS ONE

And the lawless one the antichrist will be revealed and the Lord Jesus will slay him with the breath of His mouth and brings him to an end by his appearing at His coming.

THE ANTICHRIST

Who is such a liar who denies that Jesus is the Christ (the Messiah)? He is antichrist (the antagonist of Christ) who habitually denies and refuses to acknowledge the father and the son.

THE BEAST

A Reed (is a measuring rod) was then given to me shaped like a staff, and I was told: Ride up and measure the sanctuary of God and the altar of incense and number those who worship there. (Revelation 11:1)

He brought me there, and behold, there was a man (an angel) whose appearance was like bronze with a line of flax and a measuring reed in his hand, and he stood in the gateway. And the man said to me, son of man look with your eyes and hear with your eyes and hear with your ears, and set your hearts and mind on all that I will show you, for you are brought here that I may show them to you. Declare all that you see to the house of Israel.

Then I saw another beast rising up out of the land (itself) he had two horns like a lamb, and the spoke roared like a dragon. He exerts all the powers and rights of control of the former beast in his presence and causes the earth and those who dwell upon it to exalt and deify the first beast whose deadly wounds was healed and to worship him.

CHARACTERISTICS OF THE ANTICHRIST

(1) He will be highly intelligent Daniel 8:23-25 and in the later time of their kingdom , when the transgressors are come to the full, a king of fierce countenance, and understanding dark sentences, shall stand up. And his power: shall be might, and but not by his own power: and prosper and practice, and shall destroy the policy also he shall cause craft to prosper in his hand and he. Shall magnify himself on his heart and by peace shall he stand up against the prince of princess but shall be broken without hand.

(2) He will be a great Orator Revelation 13:2; 5-6 And the beast which I saw was like unto a leopard and his feet were as the feet of a dear, and his mouth as the mouth of a lion and the dragon gave him his power and his seat and great authority and there was given unto him a mouth speaking greater things and blasphemies and power was given unto him to continue forty and two months he opened his mouth in blasphemy against God. To blasphemy in his name and his tabernacle, and them that dwell in heaven. The bible says that the king shall do according magnify himself above every god and shall speak marvelous things against God of gods and shall prosper till the indignation be accomplished: for that, that is determined shall be done.

(3) He will have a great understanding of Human philosophy and theology. Read Revelation 13:5-6

THESE ARE TWENTY FOLD POWER OF THE ANTICHRIST

(1) Blaspheme: God Daniel 7:8 "I considered the horns and behold there up among them an-other little horn before whom there were three of the first horns plucked up by the roots and be hold in this horn were eyes like a man and a mouth

speaking great things the little horn came up last after the ten (10). Horns were fully grown it plucked up three (3) of their ten (10) horns by the roots symbolizing the antichrist coming in the days of the fornication of Rome—into kingdoms, He will over throw three of them and others will be submit to him with-out further war. See Dan. 18:23- 24

(2)   Overcome Saints: Daniel 7:21-22 I behold, and the same horn made war with the saints, and prevailed against them. Until the Ancient of days came and judgment was given to the saints of the Most High and the time came that the saints possessed the kingdom. In Revelation chapter twenty from verse four the Bible says "And I saw thrones, and they sat upon them, and judgment was given unto them and I saw the souls of them that were beholden for the witness of Jesus and for the Word of God and which had not worshipped the beast, neither his image, neither hands and they lived and reigned with Christ a thousand years.

SIX REASONS FOR BEHOLDING
(1)   For the witness (testimony of Jesus.)
(2)   For the Word of God.
(3)   Not for worshipping the beast.
(4)   Not for worshipping his image.
(5)   For not taking his mark upon their foreheads.
(6)   For not taking his mark upon their hands.

OVERCOME JEWS
The Bible says in Revelation chapter twelve from verses thirteen to seventeen (Revelation 12:13-17) "And when the dragon saw that he was cast unto the earth, he persecuted the woman which brought forth the man child. And to the woman were eagle that she might fly into the wilderness, into her place, where she is nourished for a time and times and half a time

from the face of the Serpent. And the Serpent cast out of his mouth water as a flood after the woman, that he might cause her to be carried away of the flood. And the earth helped the woman, and the earth open her mouth and swallowed up the flood which the dragon cast out of his mouth. And the dragon was worth with the woman and went to make war with the remnant of her seed. Which keep the commandments of God, and have the testimony of Jesus Christ." Proofs of the woman of symbol of Israel. By the term Israel we mean Israel nation or Israel as a nation. Not a scattered among the nations, Israel now has been a nation since 1948. Many Jews will continue in all lands until they are completely gathered at the Second Advent (Matthew 24:29-31).

Immediately after the tribulation of those days the sun will be darkened and the moon will not shed its light, and the stars will fall from the sky, and the powers of the heavens will be shaken then the sign of the Son of man will appear in the sky, and then all the tribes of the earth will mourn and beat their breast and lament in anguish, and they will see the Son of Man coming in the clouds of heaven with power and great glory (in brilliancy and splendor) And He will send out His angels with a loud trumpet call, and they will gather His elect. (His chosen ones) from the four winds, (even) from one end of the universe to the other.

And it shall be in that day that a great trumpet will be blown, and they will come who were lost and ready to perish in the land of Assyria and those who were driven out to the land of Egypt, and they will worship the Lord on the holy mountain of Jerusalem.

And the Lord shall be seen over them and His arrow shall go forth as the lighting, and the Lord God will blow the trumpet and will go forth in the windstorms of the south.

And every one who is left of all nations which come against Jerusalem shall even go up from year to year to worship the king, the Lord of hosts and to keep the feast of Tabernacles or Booths.

The seventh angel then blew (his) trumpet, and there were mighty voices in heaven, shouting. The dominion (kingdom, sovereignty, rule) of the world has now come into possession and become the kingdom of our Lord and His Christ (the Messiah) and He shall reign forever and ever (for the eternities of the eternities.

Revelation chapter nineteen from verse fifteen (19:15) and out of his mouth goeth a sharp sword that with it he should smile the nations: and he shall rule them with a rod of iron: and he treads the winepress of the fierceness and wrath of the Almighty god. I behold and the same horn made war with the saints and prevailed against them until the Ancients of days came, and judgment was given to the saints of the most high, and the time came that the saints possessed the Kingdom (Daniel 7:21-22)

Chapter Ten

The Conquer Of Many Nations.

The Bible says I considered the horn and behold there came up among them another little horn before whom there were three of the first horns, plucked up by the roots and behold in this horn were eyes like the eyes of man and a mouth speaking great things. In Daniel chapter seven from verses twenty-three and twenty four (Dan. 7:23-24). The Bible says thus (the angel) said, the fourth beast shall be the fourth kingdom on earth, which shall be different from all other kingdoms and shall be different from all other kingdoms and shall devour the whole earth, tread it down, break it in pieces and crush it. And for the ten horns, of this ten kingdoms shall arise ten kings, and another shall arise after them, and he shall be different from the former ones, and he shall subdue and put down the three kings and he shall speak words against the most high (God) and shall wear out the saints of the most High (God) and think to change the time) of sacred feast and the holy days) and the law and the saints shall be given into his hands for a time, two times, and half a time (three and half years) (see Revelation 13:1-6).

The little horn came up at last after the ten horns were fully grown. It plucked up three of the ten by the roots symbolizing the Antichrist, coming in the days of the formation of Rome into ten kingdoms. He will overthrow three and others will submit to him without further war.
Revelation chapter 17 from Verses 11 to 17 (Revelation 17: 11-17) and the beast that was, and is not, even he is the eight and is of the seventh and goeth in perdition. And the ten horns which

thou sawest are ten kingdoms which have no kingdoms as yet; but receive power as kings one hour with the beast. These have one mind, and shall give their power and strength unto the beast. These shall make war with the 'Lamb' and the lamb shall overcome them. For He is the Lord of Lords and king of kings: and they that are with him are called and chosen, and faithful. And he said unto me, the waters which thou sawest where the whore sitteth, are peoples, multitude and nations and tongues. And the ten horns which thou sawest upon the beast, these shall hate the whore and make her desolated and hacked, and shall eat her flesh, and bum her with fire. For God hath in their heart to fulfill his will and to agree and to give their kingdom unto the beast, until the words of God shall be fulfilled.

Antichrist the white horse rider in Revelation 6:2 is not the same with white horse rider in Revelation 19:11-21. The reader of the two must know the difference between the two, the reader must not confused him/herself. This one is symbolical and the other one is literal. The white horse Revelation chapter six from Verse two (6:2) represent the Anti-Christ, and the other which the Bible tell us in Revelation 19:11-21 is Christ Jesus in person. This one begins a series of terrible events on the earth. The one in Revelation. 19:11-21 ends these events.

And I looked, and saw there a white horse whose rider carried a bow. And a crown was given him, and he rode forth conquering and to conquer (Revelation 6:2). This rider is the antichrist (see Zechariah 1:8-11) I saw by night and behold a man riding upon a red horse, and he stood among the myrtle tree that were in the bottom, and behind him were there red horses speckled, and white. They said I, Oh my Lord what are these? And the angel that talked with me said unto me, I will show thee what these be.

And the man that stood among the myrtle trees answered and said, these are they whom the Lord as hath sent to walk to and from through the earth. And they answered the angel of the Lord that stood among the myrtle trees, and said, we have walked to and fro through the earth and behold the earth sitteth still, and is at rest.

Furthermore this white horse rider is not a symbol of a great revival of the word of God, as some teach from Habakkuk 3:8-9 which is in the past tense and refers to God leading Israel out of Egypt. This rider is future and will be the first. Sixty- two (62) post rapture events of Daniel's Seventieth week (70) of years seven proofs of this rider is Antichrist (Revelation 6:2)

(1) An individual is referred to (verse 2).

(2) He comes on the white horse, imitating Christ and claiming to be him Verse 2. Matthew 24:4-5, and Jesus answered and said unto them take heed that no man deceive you. For many shall come in my name, saying, I am Christ, and shall deceive many.

Daniel. 9:27 and he shall confirm the covenants with many for one week, and in the midst of the week he shall cause the sacrifice and the oblation to cease, and for the over spreading of the abominations he shall make it, desolate, even until the consummation, and that determined shall be poured upon the desolate. (See Daniel 11:37). He shall regard neither the God of his fathers nor the desire of women, nor regard any god, for he shall exalt himself above all them all.

(3) A bow in symbolic language in connection with man pictures evil designs and conquest Psalm 7:12, 11:2, Psalm 37:14 Jeremiah 49:35 Christ is always symbolized having a sword, not a bow (Revelation. 1:16 He had in His right hand seven stars, out of His mouth went a sharp two edged sword, and His countenance was like the sun shining in its strength Revelation. 19:15-21).

(4) Scriptures makes it clear that Satan is the one who gives Antichrist a crown (Daniel 8:24; Daniel 11:38-39. Revelation. 13:2-4.

(5) Antichrist in the only person predicted in scripture as going forth conquering and conquer at this particular time, beginning the Daniel 7; 7-8, 20 - 24, 8:23-24, Dan. 9:27, 11:36 - 45, Revelation 6:1) It takes him the first three and half years (3 1/2) of the 70th week or seventy years of this age to get power over the first ten kingdom (10) inside the Roman empire territory. He will first over throws the three (3) of them. Daniel 7:23-24). Then by the middle of the week the ten (10) kings submit to, him without further war. He then reigns over ten kingdoms for three and half
Years and fights Christ Jesus at Armageddon, Revelation.13:1-5, Revelation 17:8-17, Revelation.19:11-21.

(6) The rider of the white horse will cause the wars, famines, pestilences', death, and hell of the following three seats (Revelation. 6:3-8).

(7) If this is not Antichrist, then we do not have mentioned in Revelation before the middle of the week (Revelation 13) were that the case, we should have two men going forth to conquer at the beginning of the week. One clearly pictures in Daniel chapter seven from verses twenty- three and twenty four. Daniel. 2:23-24, 8:23-25 and one here, without these passages in Daniel the sphere of conquest, the numbers of nations conquered, the identity of the conquers, and his rise to power, and other facts could be defined but putting these passages with Revelation 6:1-2, 13:1- 8, 14:9-21, 16:13-16, Revelation. 17:1-17.

We have the complete revelation of the one man, if we do not take the one in Daniel and the one here as being identical, then we can know nothing regarding the identity of the white horse rider.

(a) Wonder why did you wonder Verse 6-7? The beast caries her, so she must be something separate from the beast itself. One is political and other religious. The beast has seven heads (7) and ten horns (10). He is not anyone with heads and horns.

DESTROY MYSTICAL BABYLON:
Rev. 17:12-17

(1) Playing the whore is symbolic language always refers to religious fornication and idolatry Isaiah 23: 17.

(2) He, causing many nations to commit fornication with her. Proves that idolatrous religious practices.

(3) She is not a political power for she is not classed as one with kings of the earth. She only causes the kings and inhabitants of the earth to be drunk with the wine of her fornication. Since fornication here refer to religious harlotry then her influence over the nations through religion. The beast of the woman rides is the 8th Kingdom made up of the many waters or people inside the old Roman Empire territory since the beast itself is the kingdom the woman must be religious dominating the kingdom until it is destroyed. Revelation 17:12-17).

The attire of the great whore identifies her as a religious system or a whore committing spiritual fornication, duping, political power by her whoredom and idolatries (Rev. 17:4). The purple, scarlet precious stones, pearls, and golden vessels indicate the wealth of the system.

The golden cup in her hand, full of her uncleanness spiritual fornication. The abomination but which she dupes political powers proves her to be religious power. The name mystery Babylon indicates she is not literal Babylon. The word mystery identifies her with the religious rites and mysteries of ancient Babylon.

HOW BABYLON IS TO BE DESTROYED
(1)   By an earth quake (Rev. 16:17-21)
(2)   By a supernatural destruction (Rev. 18:8)
(3)   Suddenly in one hour (Rev. 18:8-19)
(4)   By fire from heaven (Rev. 18:8-19 Isa. 13:1
(5)   By the earth swallowing her (Rev. 18:21)
(6)   By God as He destroyed Sodom. Jeremiah 50:40, Isa. 13:19

Chapter Eleven

The Two Witnesses and Their Mission.

The Bible tells us plainly in Revelation 11; 7-12 that and when they shall have finished their testimony, the beast that ascended out of the bottomless pit shall war against them, and shall overcome them, and kill them. And their dead bodies shall lie in the streets of the great city which spiritually is called Sodom and Egypt, where also our Lord is crucified. And they of the people and kindred have and tongues and nations shall see their dead bodies to be put in graves. And they that dwell upon the earth shall rejoice over them and make merry, and shall send gifts one to another because these two prophets tormented them that dwelt on the earth. And after three days and half the spirit of life from God entered into them and they stood upon their feet, and great fear fell upon them which saw them. And they heard a great voice from heaven.

Who are the two witness?

The two witnesses are two men not two covenants or dispensations. They are Christ's witnesses and they will be given power in the future when they come to the earth. The two men will be prophets, they will prophesy for the last forty-two (42) Months or 1,260 days 3 1/2 years of Daniel 70th week. They will be clothed in sackcloth, they are symbolized by two olive tree and two candle sticks which stands before God, Zechariah 4:11-14 "then answered I, and said unto him what are these two olive trees upon the right side of the candlestick and upon the left side thereof? I answered again and said unto him, what be these two olive branches which through the two unto him, what be these two olive branches which through the two golden pipes empty the golden oil out of themselves. And he answered me and said, knowers thou not what these be? And I said, o my Lord Then he said by the Lord of the whole earth. The two witnesses were already in heaven when Zachariah prophesied, and about five hundred (500) years before Christ came physically to this earth. John the beloved saw the two witnesses in heaven about 96 AD. So who so ever they are two witnesses are two men translated to heaven at least five hundred years before Christ came to this earth. Hence the two witnesses can't be John the Baptist, John the Beloved, not one of the Apostles, or any other man living after five hundred years before Christ Jesus (500BC).

The two witnesses will be invincible for the three and half years 3 1/2) of their ministry Revelation 11:5-7)" If any man will hurt them fire proceeded out of their mouth and devoured their enemies, If any man will hurt them he must in this manner be killed. These has power to shut heaven, that it rain not in the days of their prophecy, and have power over waters to turn them to blood and to smile the earth will all plagues, as often as they will. And they shall finished their testimony the beast that ascended out of the bottomless pit shall make war against them and shall overcome them and kill them. They will have power to destroy their enemies, the same way their enemies will seek to destroy them. They will be able to cause fire to come out of their mouth to destroy their enemies, they will have power to stop rain all day of their prophecy. The two witnesses will have power to turn water into blood and the earth with plagues as often as they will put when 1260 days ministry is finished the supernatural angelic spirit out abyss will use human Anti-Christ to kill them. This point seems to exclude Moses or any man who has already died as one of the witnesses, since it is appointed unto man to die as one of the witnesses, since it is appointed unto man to die once but after which cometh judgment. Hebrew 9:27. But the two will die in the hand of the Anti-Christ in the future. Hence it is certain that the two witnesses are men who have never died so that they can die at the hand of the Antichrist in the future. The two witnesses will remain dead for three and half days and then be resurrected, immortal, men when they came from heaven to begin their ministry. I King 18:21 And Elijah came to all the people, and said, how long will you falter between two opinions? If the lord is God, follow him, but if Baal, follow him, but the people answered him not a word. Then Elijah said to the people, I am alone I'm left a prophet of the Lord, but Baal's prophets are four hundred and fifty men. Therefore let them give us two bulls and let them choose one bull for themselves, cut in pieces, and lay it on the wood, but put no fire under it, and I will prepare the other bull, and lay it on the wood, but put no fire under it. Then you call on the name of your gods, and I will call on the name of the Lord, and the God who answered by fire, He is God. So all the people answered and said, it is well spoken. Now Elijah said to the prophets of Baal, choose one bull for yourselves, and prepare it first, for you are many, and call on the name of your god, but put no fire under it. And so it was at noon that Elijah mocked them and said, cry aloud, for he is a god, either he is meditating, or he is busy, or he is on a journey, or perhaps, he is sleeping and must be awakened. So they cried aloud, and cut themselves, as was their custom, with knives and lances, until the blood gushes out on them.

Then Elijah said to all the people, come here to me, so all the people came near to him. And he repaired the altar of the Lord that was broken down. And Elijah took twelve stones, according to the number of the tribes of the sons of Jacob, to whom the word of the Lord had come, saying Israel shall be your name. Then with the stones he built an altar in the name of the Lord, and he made a trench around the altar large enough to hold two seat of seed. He put the wood in order, cut the bull in pieces, and laid it on the wood, and said fill four water pots with water and pour it on the burnt sacrifice and on the wood. That the prophet Elijah came near and said, Lord God of Abraham, Isaac and Israel, let it be known this day that you are God in Israel and I am your servant, and that I have done all these things at your world. Then the fire of Lord fell and consumed the burnt sacrifice and the wood and the stones and the dust, and it licked up the water that was in the trench.

When the people saw it they fell on their faces, and they said, The Lord, He is God, The Lord he is God. Elijah said to them seize the prophets of Bad, do not let one of them escape, so they seize them and Elijah brought them down to the Brook Kishon and execute them there.

Elijah challenged the Prophet of Baal also John the Baptist challenged the Pharisees (See Luke 3:7-10). All the prophetic scholars agree that Elijah will be one of the witnesses, some scholars, however argue that the other witness will be Enoch while some argue that the other witness will be Moses.

The Bible predicted Elijah as one of the two witness (Malachi 4:5) Behold I will send you Elijah the prophet before coming of the great and dreadful day of the Lord. He shall turn the heart of the fathers to the child and the heart of the children to the fathers, lest I come and smites the earth with a curse.

John the Baptist was not Elijah. John 1:21. They asked him, what then? Art thou Elias? He said I am not. Art thou the prophet? He answered NO. He only came in the spirit and power of Elijah to prepare the hearts of men for the Messiah's first coming (first Advent) the way that Elijah will prepare their hearts for the second coming of the Messiah Luke 1:17. Basic similarities between Elijah and John the Baptist.
(1) Elijah challenged the Prophets of Baal 1 Kings 18:21 also John the Baptist challenged the Pharisees Luke 3:7-10.

(2) Elijah accused king Ahab of the injustice and murder of Naboth 1 Kings 21:20 so also John the Baptist accused King Herod of Committing adultery with his brother's wife Matthew 14:4.

(3) Elijah used to live in the wilderness Isaiah 40:3 I Kings 19:4 also John the Baptist too lived in the wilderness Mathew. 3:1-3.

(4) Elijah went or crossed Jordan 1 Kings 17:3 so also was Matthew 3:6 John the Baptist, he baptized people in River Jordan but he didn't cross it. Basis difference between Prophet Elijah and John the Baptist.

(a) Elijah did some miracles 1 Kings 18:30-40. 2 Kings 2:8 (15 miracles) was performed through Elijah but John the Baptist did not work any.

(b) Elijah did not die rather taken away by chariot of fire 2 Kings 2:11 while John the Baptist was be-headed Matthew 14:10

(c) The parents of Elijah were not known 1 Kings 17:1 while that of John the Baptist were known Luke 1:1-13

This really proves that John the Baptist was not Elijah. Those in the favor of Enoch argue that, the only other man translated that he see death apart from Elijah and Enoch were prophets of Judgment Jude 14).

1. Enoch also the seventh from Adam, prophesied of these, saying, Behold the Lord cometh with

ten thousands of his saints, to execute judgment upon all and to convince all that are ungodly among them of all their ungodly deeds which they _ have ungodly committed, and of all their hard speeches which ungodly sinners have spoken against him.

    She said unto Elijah what have I to do with thee O man of God? Art thou come unto me to call my sin to remembrance, and to slay my son? 1 Kings 17:18. Both must come back and die their own appointed death on earth as all men who live before the rapture. The lives of Elijah and Enoch were parallel in every sense, to their cases rise and fall together as to being the two witnesses. If either Enoch of Elijah had been translated in immortal glorified bodies they would have been the first fruits of the resurrection instead of Christ 1 Corinthians 15:20-23) but both Enoch and Elijah are in heaven in their natural bodies and they return to fulfill the predictions in Revelation 11:1-6 Then I was given a reed like a measuring rod. And the angel stood, saying, rise and measure the temple of God, the altar, and those who worship there. But leave out the court which is outside the temple, and do not measure it, for it has been given to the Gentile. And they will tread the holy city underfoot for forth-two months. And I will give power to my two witnesses, and they will prophesy one thousand two hundred and sixty days, clothed in sackcloth. These are the two olive trees and the two lampstands standing before the God of the earth. And if anyone wants to harm them, fire proceeds from their mouth and devours their enemies. And if any wants to harm them, he must be killed in this manner. These have power to shut heavens, so that no rainfall in the days of their prophecy, and they have power over waters to turn them to blood, and to strike the earth with all plagues, as often as they desire.

    Scholars who are in favor of Moses as the other witness argue that Enoch belonged to another age the antediluvian period. The most powerful argument against Enoch's being one of the witnesses is that as Hebrews declares "he was translated that he should not see death." It appears therefore that Enoch was a type ruptured church which like him shall never see death I Thessalonians 4: 13-17.

    Moses ministry in the books of Exodus was initiated when God sends him to pronounce the great plague upon

Egypt. It is said the two witnesses that they have same power that Moses had during Exodus see (Revelation 11:5-6).

This make the evidence stronger Moses and Elijah in this scene which foreshadowed the coming of the Kingdom of God actually takes places at the resurrection of the two witnesses Revelation 11:12-15).

The one reason, however that seems to disqualify Moses from being the other witnesses is that Moses died. It seems incompatible with scriptural teaching that a believer should die twice and resurrected twice. but was Moses actually or really resurrected or he just raised physically from the dead. Other Old Testament characters were. For example Elijah's raising the widow's son was Moses raised in physical rather than a glorified body? If Moses was just raised physically from the dead, as for example Lazarus was, then it is possible that Moses could be the other of the two witnesses. Although Moses died and was buried as the Bible plainly describe. It could well be that Moses raised again in his physical body, rather than a glorified body. There are certain circumstances that seem to show that this was the actual case. Moses was seen on the transfiguration with Elijah. It must have been that he had a physical body like Elijah had. How could he have? had a glorified body when Jesus Christ had not yet died and been resurrected? Christ couldn't have become the first fruit of them that slept. (1 Corinth 15:20).

Moses therefore must have been physically raised from the dead and taken to heaven as Elijah was. Moses had some very unusual experiences; his body received a remarkable quickening of divine powers on Mount Sinai so that his face shone with God's glory (Exodus 34:29-34). This remarkable experience of Moses apparently foreshadowed something that God was going to do for him later on. Just as Elijah probably experience physical transportation before he was translated I kings 18:12. So Moses received a special transfiguration, something similar to which Christ experienced. This seems to be further confirmation that something remarkable happened to Moses by the fact that, from that time on Moses did not seem to age. Although all the other Israelites who were older than twenty years died in the wilderness; Moses lived without experiencing the natural deterioration of age.

At one hundred and twenty years (120) his eyesight was still as good as ever and there was no abating of his human strength. (Deut. 34:7). What happened to Moses death is another remarkable circumstance involving the possibility that he was raised from the dead but not resurrected. If Moses was raised from the dead with his physical but not a glorified body, then the event probably happened within a few days after his death before physical corruption set in. This could not have been done if the children of Israel had buried Moses.

They would have embalmed him as they did Joseph (Genesis 50:26) for thirty days they would have had the body before them in the mourning (Deuteronomy 34:9). Indeed they would have certainly taken the body of Moses that he would not go. Therefore, God did something for Moses that he did for no one else. He buried Moses by Himself (Deut. 34:6). His life was attempted at birth, he tried to deliver his brethren but was rejected as Christ was rejected, He took a gentile bride as Christ did, he was called of God to redeemed Israel as Christ was; Moses fed the children of Israelites with Manna, a type of bread of life which Christ gave; he fasted on the mount for forty days and nights as Christ, his face shone on the mount as Christ shone on the mount of transfiguration, he was great intercessor as Christ Jesus, he was meek as Christ was Meek. He raised the brazen Serpent in the wilderness which was a type of Christ's being raised up from His death.

Moses body did not remained in the grave, although the devil evidently used his power to keep it there God sent Michael the archangel to see that Moses body was raised Jude said yet Michael the archangel when contending with the devil he disputed about the body of Moses dust not bring against him a railing accusation, but said, "the Lord rebuke thee."

It is evident that Moses was raised; Michael would not have to fight Satan and live it in the grave. Hence it is evidence that Moses received back a preserved physical body rather than fully glorified body. Moses could not receive a glorified body as Christ received at his resurrection since Christ is the first fruit of the resurrection

Chapter Twelve

The Time and Length of the Tribulation.

WAR IN HEAVEN

And then shall the tabernacles of his palace between the seas in the glorious holy mountain, yet he shall come to his end, and more shall help him. Daniel. 12:1. And at that time shall Michael stand up, the great prince which standout for the children of thy people, and there shall be a time of trouble, such as never was since there was a nation even to that same and at that time thy people shall be delivered, every one that shall found written in the book of life. There is going to be war in heaven as predicted in Revelation Chapter Twelve Revelation. 12:7-9). And there was war in heaven Michael and his angels fought against the dragon; and the dragon fought and his angels, and prevailed not, neither was there a place found any more in heaven. And the great dragon was cast out, that old serpent called the Devil and Satan; which deceived the whole world, he was cast out into the earth and his angels were cast out with him. This war in heaven will be the last actual struggle between Satan and God over the possession of the heaven, the atmosphere heaven. This war will be taken place in the middle of Daniel's seventieth week in the heaven over the possession of heaven where Satan reigns. When Satan rebelled against in the dateless past, before the six day of the creation of the earth he was cast down with a third of God's angel that rebelled with him. Some of these demons are bound now in chains awaiting for judgment (II Peter 2:4). These ones are in Tartarus, (Tar taros) Greek, Tartarus Latin, is dark abyss a place of punishment. It is a prison of angels, located under the earth.

Tartarus is a place of confinement for angels until judgment Revelation 20: 11-15.
It is a place of darkness and an eternal fire and vengeance. In the Greek fables and writings lower than has (grave) where the Titans supposed to be the first children of the earth and even older than the Greek gods. Were cast when they lost their war with Zeus.

Bible scholars believe that the Tartarus was a place visited by Christ when he died and was buried, he went to hell to take back the keys which Satan took from Adam and Eve. (Psalm 16:10 and I Peter 3:9). These Scholars argued that Christ by Holy Spirit anointing preached to the angels in Tartarus while his body was in the grave, other scholars, however disagree with this notion. These argued that Christ could not have preached, to fallen angels since angels are non-redemptive creatures (Jude 6:7). And the angels which kept not their first estate but left their own habitation, he hath reserved in everlasting chains under darkness unto judgment of the great day. Even as Sodom and Gomorrah and even the cities about them in the like manner, giving themselves over to fornication, and going after strange flesh are set forth far an example suffering the Vengeance of eternal life.

Satan is not in hell now, he is still accuser of the brethren and reigns as a prince of the air, in the atmospheric heaven while the great tribulation is going on in earth at the middle of Daniel's seventieth week, Archangel Michael and his angels will engage Satan and his demons on a fierce battle over the possession of the atmospheric heavenliest. According to the Revelation (12:7-8) one army of angels is going to defeat Satan and his army of demons to this earth. The defeated army of demons will be tormented forever. Matthew 24:41, Rev. 20: 10.

We must not forget, however that war in heaven predicted in Revelation 12:7-9 is different from that of Isaiah 14:12-14, Luke 10:18 that one of Isaiah was fought in heaven in the dateless past, before the six days work of Genesis 1:3 and Genesis 2:25. The very war predicted in Revelation is yet to take place in heaven (in future). All these things must be after the Church raptured

RISE AND REIGN OF ANTICHRIST

Bible Scholars believe that the Antichrist is the prince that shall come recorded in Daniel Chapter 9:26-27. After threescore and two weeks shall Messiah be cut off, but not for himself, and the people of the prince that shall come shall destroy the city and the sanctuary, and the end thereof shall be with a flood and unto the end of the war dissolutions are determined. He shall confirm the covenant with many for one week, and in the midst of the week he shall cause the sacrifices and the oblation to cease, and for the overspreading of abominations he shall make it desolate and that determined shall be poured upon the desolate. According to the prophecy, when the prince who shall come will make a covenant with the Jews for a week or seven years and the Jews will begin the offerings again, In the middle of the week however, he shall break the covenant and cause the sacrifice and oblation to cease if the Jews are to start their sacrifice and offerings once more, it will be in the temple.

The question is now generally raised is how can the Jews rebuild their temple, when a Muhammad mosque, the mosque of Omar is present, occupying where the old Temple of Solomon used to be? The general assumption is that the mosque of Omar will some ways be removed.

How will this be done? Many Scholars believe that building the temple is close to the Muslims mosque is most unlikely. Since such a reconstruction may trigger a Muslim holy war. Base in this assumption, the Bible scholars suggested that Iran and the Muslim world, will join forces with Russia to fight against Israel before the battle of Armageddon. Another suggestion is that a great synagogue (completed in 1981) which built about a mile west of the Temple. The Bile scholars may make whatever assumption they like but one fact is practically true, the temple of Solomon must be rebuilt either prior to or during the tribulation. How and when I don't know, but it's certain that the antichrist will defile the Jewish Temple (Matthew 24:15, Dan 9:26- 27).

The Antichrist will be a man, who claims to be God, he will imitate Christ. He will be a deceiver, the mystery of iniquity which will not be revealed till the rapture of the church. The Antichrist will be a great delusion and a liar, he will be Satan's agent and his last attempt to raise up a world dictator, immediately after the rapture of the Church the world will enter into a period of the great Tribulation.

The great tribulation will also for seven days of years. During the first three and a half years of the great tribulation, Russia (Maggog) according to some writers will move to fight against Israel but through the miracles of Gods intervention Russia and her alliance will be defeated. Also immediately after the rapture, a political figure or world leader rises to power and blasphemes God. This fellow, known as Antichrist will come as a very brilliant politician (an amazing man, a sort of man Mr. know all, who has the answers to every problem, be its political, economic, Religious etc. He will come as a man of peace and within a few years because many nations of the world to unit.

The religious, multitudes who missed the rapture, because of unbelief, will merge into a super world religious system. This world religious movement or great whore of Revelation will corporate totally, with the Antichrist to give him their support and loyalty.

The beginning of the reign of the Antichrist will be a time of great safety and prosperity (Pseudo) peace will be present everywhere. With the aid of computers, the Antichrist will be able to control everyone on the globe. Suddenly, at the middle of his reignite of the Antichrist will change and reveal himself as an embodiment of lawlessness. He will cause the whole world to get a certain mark six hundred and sixty six (666) on their forehead or on their right hand. Without this mark none will be able to buy and sell anything. Read Revelation 13:16-18. "And he caused all small and great, rich and poor, and free and bond, to receive the mark in their right hand or their foreheads. And that no man might buy and sell, save he that no man mark or the name of the beast or the number of his name. Here is wisdom. Let him that hath understanding count the number of the beast for it is the number of man and his number is six hundred and sixty six or hundred threescore and six (666)." The Antichrist will be a religious man. His religious leader will be given demonic powers to perform miracles, to cause fire to come down from heaven and to command the image of the Antichrist to become a living thing. The false prophet will because men to make the image of the Antichrist to be worshipped. He will have to give life to the image and to cause it to do personal acts. He will cause the image to demand death penalty for all who will not worship the Antichrist. There are three brands of the Antichrist.

(a) A mark Revelation 13:16-17, Revelation 15:2.
(b) And I saw as it were a sea of glass mingled with fire and them that had get victory over the number of his name, stand on the sea of glass having the harps of God.
(c) Revelation. 20:4-6: and I saw thrones and they sat upon them and judgment was given unto them and I saw the souls of them

that were beheaded for the witness of Jesus, and for the Word of God, and which had received not his mark upon their foreheads, or in their hands; and they lived and reigned with Christ a thousand years. But the rest of the dead lived not again until the thousand years were finished; this is the first resurrection. Blessed and holy is he that hath part in the first resurrection. On such the second death hath no power, but they shall be priests of Christ, and shall reign with him a thousand years." This may be the emblem of his kingdom, the name of the number of his name. The mark of the antichrist will be a literal brand upon the right hand of foreheads of the people. Revelation 13:16, Revelation 14:9. The name of the beast Revelation 14:11.

Revelation 14:9 and the third angel followed them, saying with a loud voice, if any man worship the beast and his image and receive his mark in his foreheads or in his hand.

Revelation 14:11 and the smoke of their torment ascended up forever and ever and they have not rest day and night who worship the beast and his image, and whosoever received the mark of his name.

The actual name of the antichrist is not stated in the scripture. The false prophet, as the executor of the Antichrist plan, will make a law that no man may buy and sell unless he or she takes one of the three brands of the antichrist (Rev. 13:17). He then causes men in the kingdom of Antichrist to take mark or the name of the Antichrist or the number of his name in the right hand or forehead.

The antichrist or the mystery six hundred and sixty six (is something that provokes theological curiosity. Critical commentators have some riddles difficult to declare concerning the Antichrist. One of such riddles is what is the extent of the reign of the antichrist?

Will the antichrist reign over the whole world. To understand the extent of the antichrist reign, we shall now treat the vision of Prophet Daniel (Daniel 7:1-28). This vision was 35 `fold vision Daniel saw four wind that strove against the great sea or Mediterranean Sea. Out of the sea came up four great beasts diverse from one another. The first beast was like a lion; the second beast like a bear, the third beast was like a leopard with four wings and four heads. The fourth beast was non descriptor, dreadful and terrible, and exceedingly strong.

This forth beast was different from others that were before it. It broke in pieces and stamped the rest of the beast with its feet. It has ten horns, but another little horn grew on its head among the ten horns. It grewth, it plucked up three of the ten horns by the roots in it (the little horn came eye like a man's and a mouth speaking great things. After this thrones were set and ancient of days did sit. His garment was white as snow his hair like pure wool, his throne like a fiery flame, and his wheels as burning fire. A fiery stream shot out from before him.

The judgment was set, innumerable persons helped him judge and innumerable others stood before him to be judged. The books were opened. The little horn spoke great words, but the beast (the fourth beast) was finally slain. His body was destroyed and given to the burning flame. The rest of the beast, however, had their dominion taken away and, before they were destroyed they counted a short time; after the destruction of the beast. The son of a man came with the clouds of heavens. He came to the ancient of days was brought before him, and the son of was given dominion, and glory and a kingdom that all nations should serve him, His dominion is eternal and His kingdom shall never be destroyed.

The beginning of the vision in symbols winds in symbolic passages denotes wars, strife; and judgments from God (Dan 7:8-13) I was considering the horns, and there was another horn, a little one, coming up among them, before whom three of the first horn were plucked out by the roots.

And there, in this horn, were eyes like the eyes of man, and a mouth speaking pompous words. I watched till thrones were put in place, and the Ancient of Days was seated, His garment was white as snow, and the hair of His head was like pure wool. His throne was fiery flame, its wheels a burning fire, A fiery stream issued and came forth from before Him, Ten thousand times ten thousand stood before Him. The court was seated and the books were opened. I watched then because of the sound of the pompous words which the horn was speaking, I watched till the beast was slain, and its body destroyed and given to the burning flame. As for the rest of the bests, they had their dominion taken away, yet their lives were prolong for a season and a time. I was watching in the night visions, and behold, one like the Son of Man, coming with clouds of heaven He came to the Ancients of Days, and they brought Him near before Him. Then to Him was given dominion and glory and kingdom, then all peoples, nations, and languages should serve Him. His dominion is an everlasting dominion, which Compared with Jeremiah 25:32-33.

    Beast in symbolic passages represents kingdoms. All these beasts or kingdoms rode out of these of people. The first beast like a lion with eagle's wings was the thirds world empire to, persecuted Israel was the kingdom of Babylon. The kingdom of Babylon is compared to a lion and the wings denote the swiftness of the conquest of Nebuchadnezzar.

The second beast a bear is fitting symbol of Medo Persia the fourth world empire because of their cruelty, thirst after blood, their robberies and love of spoil (Isaiah 13:16-18), Jeremiah 51:48-56). Tradition had it that the largest species of bear are found in the mountains of media. Persia was the great of the two kingdoms. The three ribs in the mouth of the bear symbolizes the conquest of Babylon, Libya and Egypt by the Medes Persians.

The third beast: A Leopard with the four wings of a fowl it is a fit symbol of the Grecian Empire founded by Alexander the great. The four wings of the fowl symbolize the swiftness of the Alexander's conquest. None of the conquest of the beast equaled those of Alexander. Heads in symbolic passages denotes kingdoms. The Leopard had four heads.

The fourth beast nondescript is a symbol of the old Roman Empire. The beast conquered all the territories of the others beasts Babylon, Medo-Persian, and Greece. It was different from all other beasts not only in republican form but also in power, greatness, and extent of dominion and length of duration. Horns like heads, in symbolic passages denote kingdoms. The beast had ten horns. These ten horns symbolizes ten kingdoms in the later days the last form of the Old Roman Empire (not ten Barbaric kingdoms that destroyed Rome of "between 351-474 AD".

The little horn symbolizes the Antichrist. The little horn is the same as the Beast Revelation 13:1. The Antichrist will be a leader (king of Emperor, president), of one of the ten (10) kingdoms to be formed in the territory once occupied by the Roman Empire. He will over throw three of these kingdoms, and the rest will submit to him without further wars. Once the others agree to give their powers to him, the Antichrist will become strong and form the eight (8) world empire to persecute Israel. The false prophet and the Antichrist will later be captured, slain and thrown into the lake of fire, to be tormented one thousand years (1000) before the Armageddon, will be a battle between Christ and the nations, the aim of the Antichrist is to destroy Israel but the aim of the devil will be use the nations an instrument of stopping Christ form setting up his Kingdom on earth. Just at the moment, the Messiah shall come. Jesus shall come with the clouds. The Lord Jesus shall come riding on a white horse, and the armies of heaven will come with Hm, riding with Him. Jesus will come in glory; he will

come as King of kings and Lord of lords. Jesus Christ is also called the Faithful truely, when Jesus shall appear his eyes shall be like flames of fire (Revelation 19: 11, 20: 15).
Jesus Christ will come with the armies of heaven as their commander in chief. These armies include all the redeemed and resurrected saints of all ages and all the angels of heaven (Revelation 19:14, Jude 1:14-15). God the father will also participate in the battle of Armageddon in Daniel 7:9 the ancient of days is mentioned as the one who will sit to judge the rebels.

Who is this ancient of Days? The Bible described him as one whose garment was white as snow and the hair of his head like pure wool. In days one like the son of man. This is not the clouds of heaven and came to the ancient of days. He is not the Ancient because he the son of man is brought near the ancient of days.

This shows that there are two separate persons, each having their own personal body, soul and spirit. The Ancient of days is God the Father. The bible not only teaches the first and second coming of Jesus Christ to the earth. (Daniel 7:9). I behold till the thrones were cast down and the Ancient of days did sit whose garment was white as snow, and the hair of his head like a pure wool: his throne was like the fiery flame, and his wheels as burning fire.
Zechariah 14:5. And ye shall flee to the valley of the mountains; for the valley of the mountains shall reach unto Azul: yea, ye shall flee, like as ye fled from before the earthquake in the days of Isaiah King of Judah: and the Lord my God shall come, and the entire saint with thee. Titus 2:3. Looking for that blessed hope, and the glorious appearance of the great God and our savior Jesus Christ. At this first coming, God the Father comes to help Christ defeat and destroy the Antichrist kingdom. God then gives the kingdom to the Son Jesus Christ and the Saints, and Christ and the Saint, goes back to heaven to remain for the

first one thousand years of the eternal reign of Christ Jesus until he has rid the earth of all rebellion (1 Corinthians 15:24-28) "Then cometh the end, when he shall delivered up the kingdom to God, even the Father, when he shall have put down all rule and all authority and power for he must reign, till he hath put all enemies under his feet. The last enemy that shall be destroyed is death.

For the path put all things under his feet, but when he saint all things are put under him, it is manifest that he is accepted, which did put all things under him. And when all things shall be subdued unto him, then shall the son also himself be subject unto him that put all things under him that god may be all in all." God will then move his capital city from planet heaven to the planet earth to be among with men forever.

The second coming of God the Father to the earth will be at the millennium, when Christ has rid the earth of all rebels. God will then become all in all, on earth as before the Rebellion was started by Lucifer and Adam and Eve.

"That in the dispensation of time he might gather together in one all things in Christ, both which are in heaven, and which are on earth even 8in him". Ephesians 1:10. At the Battle of Armageddon Christ will smile the nations with the sword that goes out from his mouth. In a summary the battle will take place on the earth. When the Antichrist conquers Russia, Germany, and other countries from the north and east of the ten kingdoms, and mobilized the nations at Armageddon against Jerusalem.

It will take place at the Second Advent to deliver the Jews from Antichrist; immediately after the great tribulation and after the marriage supper of the Lamb. The battle of Armageddon will take place just before the millennium when Jerusalem is surrounded by the enemies of the nations under Antichrist, at the end of this age grace.

Armageddon will not be an ordinary battle or series of battles between two sets of earthly nations. Rather, it will be one between Jesus Christ and his heavenly armies and earthly Israel on one side, and Satan and his angels (demons) and earthly armies under the Antichrist on the other side. The battle of Armageddon will be when the seals trumpets, vials have all be fulfilled, when the two witness have finish their ministry. That is one thousand years before the new heavens and earth. The battle of Armageddon will last only one day, Satan's purpose for the earth, and thus advertising Satan's impending doom.

As a result of the battle, the beast and the false prophet will be consigned to the lake of fire forever, Satan, the angels, and demons will be consigned to the abyss for thousands of years. Also Israel will be delivered and Vindicated and God eternal kingdom will be set up.
Revelation 19:11 and I saw heaven opened, and behold a white horse, and he that sat upon him was call Faithful and True, and in His righteousness he doth judge and make war.

FROM WHERE DOES THE ANTICHRIST COME?

The Prophet Daniel saw the little horn coming out of the four divisions of the Grecian Empire. Daniel 8:8, Daniel 9:21-23. Therefore, the he goat waxed very great: and when he was strong, the great horn was broken; and for it came up four notable ones toward the four winds of heaven. And out of one of them came forth little horn, which waxed exceeding great toward the South, and toward the East and toward pleasant land. And the rough goat is the king of Grecian and the great horn between his eyes is the first king. And that is being broken, whereas four stood up out of nation, but not in his power. And later time of their kingdom, when the transgressors are come to the full, a king of fierce countenance, and understanding the dark sentences, shall stand up. This was to in the later time of their kingdom and so it must yet be in the future, for these kingdoms still exist Daniel 8:23.

    These four divisions are known today as Greece, Turkey, Syria, and Egypt. In Daniel seven tell us about Antichrist coming from ten kingdoms inside the Roman Empire and if we did not have the vision of Daniel eight we could have believe that he could come from England, Holland, Belgium, France, Switzerland, Spain, Portugal, Italy, Austria, Hungary, Hugo, Slavia, Albania, or some other part of the Roman territory outside the four divisions of the Greece Empire. But since we have Daniel Chapter 8, the narrowing down of the Antichrist must limit his coming from one of the countries stated before. He cannot come from Italy, or from the Vatican, England, America, Germany, Russia, or any other country of the world other than these four countries. It is much convinced that the Antichrist would come from Syria.

The Two Witnesses and Their Mission.

Chapter Thirteen

Antichrist, the King of The North And His Functions.
ANTICHRIST, THE KING OF THE NORTH

And the king according to his will; he shall exalt himself, and magnify himself above every God, and shall speak marvelous things against the God the Gods, and shall prosper till the indignation be accomplished: For that is determined and shall be done Daniel 11:36. In the book of Daniel chapter 12:13 the Bible says But go thy way till the end be: for thou shall rest and stand in thy lot the end of the days. These two Bible verses definitely identify the Antichrist as the north (Syria) at the time of the end. The whole purpose of this vision was to show' what shall befall thy people of Israel in the later days, see from Daniel 10:14 Now I am come to make thee understand what shall befall thy people in the later days for yet the vision is for many days.

Under the last Syrian king who is foreshadowed by Antiochus-Epiphanies (Daniel 11:21, 34) and to narrow down the coming of the Antichrist, geographically, from the four divisions of Grecian to one of the Syrian division. The vision of Daniel chapter 2, and 7 were given to show the formation of the ten kingdoms inside the old Roman Empire and reveal that the Antichrist would come out of one of these ten kingdoms, and lead these nations against Christ at his Second Advent. The purpose of Daniel chapter 8 was to give additional information to that Daniel chapter 2 and 7, to narrow down the coming of Antichrist, geographically, from the ten kingdoms of the four divisions of the Grecian Empire before Antichrist comes. The purpose of the last vision (Daniel 10:1, 12 and 12:13) was to narrow down the coming of the Antichrist, Geographically, from the four divisions of the Grecian Empire to one of these divisions, the Syria and complete the visions of Daniel concerning the days and the reign of Christ the Messiah (Daniel 11:35 and 12:13) gives the third and last description of the Antichrist in Daniel

THREE GREAT FUTURE TRI-CONTINENT WARS

The first tri-continent war will be for the purpose of forming the ten kingdoms inside the Old Roman Empire territory, fulfilling Daniel 8:23, 24. The States now inside this territory will be reduced to ten kingdoms; this will require a war in Europe, Asia, and Africa and defeat of Russia who now controls part of the territory. These ten kingdoms will Reserved Roman Empire symbolized the ten toes on the image of Daniel chapter two and the ten horns of the beast of Daniel chapter 7, Rev. 12:13, 17.

The second tri-continent war will take place the ten kingdoms formed and revised by the Roman Empire and continue a short space (Rev. 17:10) the little horn or future Antichrist will come from one of these ten kingdoms and from among them to form the eight kingdoms of Rev.17:8, 17. In this second war he will overflow three of the ten kingdoms before the others submit to him see Daniel chapter (7:23, 24 and Rev. 17:12, 17).

The third tri-continent war will be after Antichrist gets power over the ten kingdoms, in the middle of Daniel's 70th week or three and half years before the second advent of Christ (Revelation 13:5).

The ten kingdoms under Antichrist will fight this third war with the countries of north and east of Roman Empire territory (Daniel chapter 11:44). When Antichrist conquers these new enemies he will lead the nations down to Jerusalem to battle and then Christ will come to defeat them at Armageddon Ezekiel 38:3, Zechariah 14, Rev. 19:11, 21.

Revelation 12:13-17 And the dragon saw that he had been cast to the earth; he persecuted the woman who gave birth to the male child. But the woman was given two wings of a great eagle that she might fly into wildness to her place, where she is nourished for a time and times and half a time (that is three years and six months 1260 days, from the presence of the serpent. So the serpent spewed water out of his mouth, like a flood after the woman that he might cause her to be carried away by the flood. But the earth helped the woman and the earth open its mouth and swallowed up the flood which the dragon had spewed out of his mouth. And the dragon was enraged with the woman and he went to make war with the rest of her off spring, who keep the commandments of God and have the testimony of Jesus Christ. And war broke out in heaven, Michael and his angels fought with the dragon, and the dragon and his angels fought, but they did not prevail, nor was a place found for them in heaven any longer. So the great dragon was cast out, that serpent of old, called the devil and Satan, who deceives the whole world. He was cast out with him. The second tri-continental war will take place after the ten kingdoms are form.

(THE THREE GREAT FUTURE TRI-CONTINENT WARS) Part Two

Head were many crowns, and a name written, that no man knew, but himself. And he was clothed with vesture dipped in the blood, and his name is called the Word of God. And the army which were in heaven followed him on white horses, clothed in fine linen white and clean. His countenance was lightning, and his raiment white as snow (Matthew 28:3).

Mary Magdalene knew Jesus and had followed him several years before Jesus Christ was betrayed, crucified, and died on the cross of Calvary buried and he was resurrected on the third day of his burial from dead and Mary was the first person to see the resurrected Christ and he was a change person, she described him that the countenance of Jesus was like lightning and he was shining and his garment was as white as snow. John the beloved was one great twelve the Apostle of the Lord Jesus Christ among of three Apostles the very inner circle John, Peter, and James.

I, John, who also am your brother and companion in tribulation and in the kingdom and patience of Jesus Christ, was in the isle that is called Patmos, for the word of God, and for the testimony of Jesus Christ. It was on this island where the Lord Jesus revealed himself and the mystery of the Church to him. John said he was in the Lord's day and heard behind him a voice like great trumpet saying to him, I am Alpha and Omega, the first and the last what you see. Write in the book and send it unto the seven churches which are in Asia, unto Ephesians, and unto Smyrna, and unto Pergamum, and unto Thyatira, and unto Sardis, Philadelphia, and unto Laodicea. In the book of Revelation chapter 1, verses 13, the word of God say. And in midst of the seven candlesticks one like the son of man, clothed with a garment down to the foot, and girt about the golden girdle.

John said Jesus was in the midst of heaven candlesticks which are the Church of the Lord; he was in the middle of his church. And he had in his right hand seven stars and out of his mouth went a sharp two edged sword and his countenance was as sun shines in his strength. John the Apostle saw Jesus Christ whose countenance was as the sun shine and the seven Angels of the churches in his right hand this means he is the book of Daniel 7:9. I beheld till the thrones were cast down, and the ancient of the days did not sit, whose garment was as white as snow, and the hair of his head like the pure wool; his throne was like the fiery flame and his wheels as burning fire.

Prophet Daniel had this vision six hundred years before Jesus Christ was born physically on this earth, but what the Apostle John saw about Jesus Christ was the same vision of the prophet Daniel, he described him as the Ancient of days and John heard him said I am the Alpha and the Omega, the First and the Last. And out of his mouth goes a sharp sword, that with it he should smith the nations and he shall rule with rod of iron, and he treaded the winepress of the fierceness and he hath on his vesture and on his thigh a name written, KING of KINGS, and the LORD of LORDS. And I saw an angel standing in the sun, and he cried with a loud voice saying to all the fowls that fly in the midst of heaven, come gather your selves together unto the supper of the great God; that ye may eat the flesh of kings, and the flesh of captains, and the flesh of the mighty men, both free and bond both small and great.

(THE THREE GREAT FUTURE TRI-CONTINENT WARS) Part Three

Thus, the king of the north (Syria) will war on the countries of north and east of Syria, and they will be defeated, the Antichrist will go forth with great fury to destroy, and utterly make away many. Many, if not all the nations from north and east of the Roman Empire territory, and will unite to put down this new conqueror who in three and half short years will have gained complete mystery of all the ten kingdoms of the Roman Empire territory releasing. He is set upon complete world conquest they will know that they must defeat him or be defeated eventually by him, so before he recovers from his bloody wars inside the Roman Empire, they will unite to put an end to these conquests. Antichrist could perhaps conquer more of the world if it were not for Christ coming to earth to save Israel when the half of Jerusalem is taken. Thus Antichrist dream of being a total worldwide dictator will come as far short of his goal. Christ will be one and only worldwide ruler other than Adam and Noah of the human race and Lucifer of the Angelic race. Antichrist and his deities Daniel chapter 11:37-38 neither shall he regard the God of his fathers, nor the desire of women nor regard any God for he shall magnified himself above all. But in his estate shall he honor the Gold, and silver and the precious stones, and pleasant things. He will dis-regard the God of his fathers the true God. John 5:43 I am come in my father's name, and ye receive me not; if another shall come in his own name, ye will receive. Jesus Christ made it clear that he was sent by his father who was in heaven, to this earth by his father's name, but people didn't accept him, he who is lawless. The Antichrist who will come by his own name they will accept him.

The Antichrist will honor strange gods (Revelation 13:1-18) and I stood upon the sand of the sea, and saw a beast rise up out of the sea, having seven heads and ten horns, and upon his heads the name of blasphemy. And the beast which I saw was like unto a leopard, and his mouth as the mouth of a lion, and the dragon gave him his power, and his seat and great authority. And I saw one of his heads as it were wounded to death, and his deadly wounded was healed, and the entire world wondered after the beast. And they worshipped the dragon which gave him power unto the beast, saying, who is like unto the beast? Who is able to make war with him? And there was given unto him a mouth speaking great things and blasphemies, and power was given unto him to continue forty two months. He opens his mouth in blasphemy against God, to blaspheme his name, and his tabernacle, and them that dwell in heaven. And it was given to him to make war with the saints, and to overcome them, and power him over all kindred, and tongues and nations. And all that dwell upon the earth shall worship him, whose names are not written in the book of life of the Lamb slain from the foundation of the world. If any man has an ear, let him hear. He that leaded into captivity shall go into captivity; he that killed with the sword must be killed with the sword. Hence is the patience and the faith of the saints. And I beheld another beast coming up out of the earth, and he had two horns like a Lamb, and he spike as a dragon; and he exercises all the power of the first beast before him, and causes the earth and them which dwell, therein to worship the first beast, whose deadly wound was healed. And he does great wonders, so that he makes fire come down from heaven on the earth in the sight of men.

Chapter Fourteen

Reasons Why Russian Is Not the King of the North.

RUSSIA IS NOT THE KING OF THE NORTH

Many of the people teach that Russia is the king of the North of Daniel chapter 11, but this is impossible for the following reasons:

1. Russia never was part of the old Roman Empire out of which ten kingdoms must be formed in the last days and out of Antichrist must come (Daniel 7:8,23, and 24)
2. Russia never was part of the old Grecian Empire, or the four divisions that empire after the death of Alexander the Great out of which the Antichrist must come. Daniel 8:9, 14, and 23.
3. Russia is not once referred to in the wars Daniel 11:4, 34. These were eventually fought between Syria and Egypt in the period of about one hundred and fifty years ending with the reign of Antiochus Epiphanes. Therefore, to insert Russia into the future war between the future king of the north (Syria) and the king of the south (Egypt) is adding to God's word one might as well identify United States, Britain, or any other country we want to as the king of the north as to do with Russia.
4. If Russia is the king of the north (Daniel 11:4, 45) then what countries are North Russia that will make war on Russia, fulfilling the war tidings from the north and east of the this king of the north. These are not countries of Russia that could make war on her fulfilling this verse hence Russia is entirely out of the picture in Daniel chapter 11.

5. In the past Russia boarded the Syria divisions of the old Grecian Empire, so in the formation of the ten kingdoms, this will perhaps be true of the border between Syria and Russia, hence Russia could be the only country to fulfill making war on Syria at that time, for Turkey will have made a part of the ten kingdoms of the Revised Rome under the king of the North (Daniel 7:23, 24 and Revelation 17:8, 17). The only other major fallacy about Russia is that she will invade Palestine, fulfilling Ezekiel chapter 38 and 39.

Many are the speculations regarding Russia being the country from which Antichrist comes, of her fulfilling Daniel 11:40, 45. At the end time, of the end shall the king of the South push at him; and the king of the North shall come against him like a whirlwind, with chariots, and with horsemen, and with many ships, and he shall enter into the countries, and shall overflow and pass over see Isaiah 21:1.

Ezekiel 38:4 and Revelation 9:16 he shall also enter into the glorious land and many countries shall overthrow but those shall escape out of his hand even Edom, and Moab and the Chief of the children of Ammon. He shall stretch forth his hand also upon the countries, and the land of Egypt. Libyans and Ethiopians shall be at his steps, but tidings out of the east and out of the north shall trouble him. Therefore, he shall go forth with great fury to destroy and utterly to make away many. And he shall plant the tabernacles of his place between the seas in the glorious holy mountain, yet shall come to his end, and none shall help him. And the beast was taken, and with him the false prophet that wrought miracles before him, with which he received them had received the mark of the beast, and them that worshipped his image. These were cast alive into the lake of fire burning with brimstone (Revelation 19:20) if Bible scholars will recognized one thing, not only will Ezekiel 38, and 39 be clear for them but also Daniel 11:44

That one thing is Antichrist from Syria and will get power over the ten kingdoms and revived Rome in the first three and half years of Daniel's 70th week and then war between him and his ten kingdoms and the countries east and north of the old Roman Empire territory will be fought. Antichrist will conquer the Eastern and Northern countries and become the ruler of Russia by conquest, not by being a native of Russia and coming from her. At that time he will become the god, the Chief Prince of Meshech and Tubal of at the end of this war or near the end of the last three and half years of Daniel's 70th week. Then, and then only will Ezekiel chapter 38, and 39 be fulfilled. The Antichrist will lead the newly conquered countries, together with the ten kingdoms, and other nations that will be cooperate with him, through the ministry of the three unclean spirits (Revelation 16:13, 16) to their end at Armageddon Revelation 19:11, 21 the Bible says and saw heaven opened, and behold a white horse, and he that sat upon him was called Faithful and True, and in righteousness he doth judge and make war. His eyes were as flame of fire, and on his head were many crowns, and he a name written, that no man knew, but he himself.   And at that time shall Michael stand up, the great Prince which stands for the children of your people, and there shall be a time of trouble, such as never was since there was a nation even to that same time, and at that time your people shall be delivered, every one that shall be found written in the book.

(1) At that time the Antichrist plants the tabernacle of his palace in the temple of Israel on mount Moriah.
(2) At that time Michael stands up and cast Satan and his angels to the earth to be among men.
(3) At that time the great tribulation begins in the middle of Daniel's 70th week of three and half years before the Second Advent.

(4) At that time Daniel's people are delivered (translated) every one (144,000) that shall be found written in the book of life. The tribulation will begin to affect Israel before the 70th week begins, how long before is not stated or certain, but when Antichrist rises at the beginning of the week Israel will undergoing persecution from the ten kings of the Reversed Rome dominated by Mystery Babylon. When Antichrist comes he will have a seven years covenant with Israel assuring them of protection in their continued establishment as a nation. Because the Jews will not submit to mystery of Babylon, and there will be wide spread of persecution and they shall be hated of all nations, during the beginning of sorrows when Antichrist will be endeavoring to support in his rise over these nations, so he will make alliance with them for seven years. Therefore, the time of tribulation will be the whole of Daniel's 70th week and it will end at the Second Advent of Jesus Christ.

Chapter Fifteen

The Divisions of the Tribulation

The first division takes place in the first three and half years of the 70th week and is termed the lesser tribulation. It is not to be great in severity as the last three and half years; because of the protection of Israel by the Antichrist during that time. Israel's protection then will be from a source entirely different from that of the last division. In these first three and half years she will be prosecuted by mystery Babylon and the ten kings. This division takes in the fulfillment of Revelation chapter 6:1-9, 21. And I saw when the Lamb opened one of the seals, I heard as it were the noise of thunder, one of the four beast saying, come and see, and I saw and behold white horse, and he that sat on him had a bow, and crown was given unto him, and he went forth conquering and to conquer. And when he had opened the Second seal I heard the Second beast saying come and see. And there went out another horse that was red, and power was given to him that sat thereon to take peace from the earth and that they should kill one another, and there was given unto him a great sword. And when he had opened the third seal, I heard the third beast say, come and see. And I beheld and unto a black horse, and he that sat on him had a pair of balances in his hand. And I heard a voice in the midst of the four beasts says, a measure of wheat for a penny, and three measures barley for a penny, and see that you hurt not the oil and the wine. And when he had opened the fourth seal I heard a voice of the fourth beast say, come and see. And I looked and behold a pale horse, and his name that sat on him was Death and Hell followed with him. And power was given unto them over the fourth part of the earth, to kill with sword, and hunger, and with death, and with the beast of the earth. And when he had opened the fifth seal, I saw the Altar the souls of them that were slain for the word of God and for the testimony which they held. Both Jesus, Daniel, and Jeremiah, and many others speak of this time of Israel's trouble as being worse than any other time that had ever be on the earth or ever will be.

THE PURPOSE OF THE TRIBULATION

(1) To purify Israel and bring them back to a place where God can fulfill the everlasting covenants made with their fathers.
(2) To purify Israel of all rebels (Ezekiel 20:33-34 Zechariah 13:8)
(3) To plea with and bring Israel into the bond of New Covenant (Jeremiah 30:3-11 and Malachi 4:3-4) and ye shall tread down the wicked; for they shall be ashes under the soles of your feet in the day that I shall do this, said the LORD of hosts. Remember ye the Law of Moses my servant, which I commanded onto him in Horeb for all Israel, with the statutes and Judgments
(4) To judge Israel and punished for their rejection of the Messiah and them willing to accept the Messiah be-fore he comes the second time (Matthew 24:15-31) when you therefore, shall see the abomination of dissolution spoken of by Daniel the Prophet, stand in the holy place, whose read it, let him understand then let them which be in Judea flee into the mountains and let him which is on the house top not come down to take anything out of his house. Neither let him which is in the field return back to take his clothes. And woes unto them that are with child and to them that give suck in those days. But pray you that your flight is not in the winter, neither on the Sabbath day. For then shall be great tribulation, such as was not since the beginning of the world to this time, no nor

ever shall be. And except those days should be shortened, there shall no flesh be saved, but for the elect's sake those days shall be shortened. Then, if any man shall say unto you, Lo, here is Christ, or there, believe it not. For there shall raise false Christ, and false prophets, and shall show great signs and wonders in so much that it were possible, they shall deceive the very elect. Behold I have told you before wherefore if they shall say unto you, behold, he is in the desert do not go, behold he is in the secret chambers, believe it not.

For as the lightning come out of the east, and shine even onto the west so shall also the coming of the Son of man be. For where so ever the carcass, is there where the eagles be gathered together. Immediately after the tribulation of those days, shall the sun be darkened, and the moon shall not give light and the stars shall fall from heaven, and the powers of the heaven shall be shaken. Then, shall appear the sign of the Son of Man; coming in the clouds of heaven with power and great glory. (Daniel 7:13-14) And he shall send his angels with a great sound of a trumpet, and they shall gather together his elect from the four winds, from one end of heaven to the other.

To judge nations for their persecution of Israel; who is this that comes from Edom with dyed garments from Bozrah that is glorious in his apparel traveling in the greatness of his strength? I that speak in righteousness, mighty to save wherefore art your red apparel and garment like him that trade in the wine fat?. I have treated the winepress alone with me, I will tread them in mine anger, and trample them in mine fury and their blood shall be sprinkled upon my garments and stain all my raiment. For the day of vengeance in my heart, the year of my redeemed is come to uphold therefore, mine own arm brought salvation unto me and my fury upheld me. And Joseph brought a fine linen cloth for swathing dead bodies and taking him down from the cross he rolled him up in the fine linen cloth and placed him in a tomb which had been hewn out of a rock. Then he rolled a very large stone against the door of the tomb Isaiah 53:9

Chapter Sixteen

Jesus Rose from the Dead for Us

After three days in the tomb God raised his Son from the dead. Now after the Sabbath, near dawn of the first day of the week Mary of Magdalene and the other Mary went to take look at the tomb, and behold there was great earthquake, for an angel of the Lord descended from heaven and came and rolled the boulder back and sat upon it. His appearing was like a lightning and his garments as white as snow. And those keeping guard were so frightened; at the sight of him that they were agitated and they trembled and became like dead men. But the angel said to the women, do not be alarmed and frightened, for I know that you are looking for Jesus, who was crucified. He's not here, he has risen as he said (he would do) come; see the place where he lay. Then go quickly and tell his disciples. He has risen from the dead, and behold he is going before you to Galilee, there you will see him. Behold I have told you. So, they left the tomb hastily with fear and great Joy and ran to tell the disciples. And as they went behold, Jesus met them said Hail gratings and they went to him and clasped his feet and worshipped him. Then Jesus said to them, do not be alarmed and afraid; go and tell my brothers to go into Galilee, and there they will see me. When the eleven disciples went to Galilee and saw Jesus, they fell down and worshipped him, but some doubted. Jesus approached and breaking the silence, said all power and authority in heaven and on the earth has been given to me. Go and make disciples of all nations, baptizing them in the name of the Father, and of the Son, and of the Holy Spirit. Teaching them to observe everything that I have commanded you and behold I'm with you till the end of this age.

Jesus gave power to his disciples to preach the gospel, heal the sick cast out demons, and speak in an unknown tongue. But God is so rich in his mercy because of and in order to satisfy the great and wonderful and intense love with which he love us. Even when we were dead (slain) by our own shortcoming and trespassers he made us alive together in fellowship and in union with Christ. He gave us the every life of Christ himself the same new life with which he quickened him for. It is by his grace, his favor and mercy which you did not deserve that you are saved, delivered from judgment and made partakers of Christ Salvation, and he raised us up together with him and made us sit down together, giving us joint seating with him in the heavenly sphere by virtue of our being in Christ Jesus, the Messiah the Anointed One.

JESUS OPENED THE DOOR OF HEAVEN FOR US

When his work on earth was complete, Jesus returned to heaven to be with God his Father, but this too was for us for he opened the way into God's presence for us, where we can live now and forever. Therefore, brothers, since we have confidence to enter the most holy place by the blood of Jesus, by a new living way opened for us through the curtain, that is his body. Let us draw near to God with a sincere heart in full assurance of faith. Do not let your hearts be troubled (distressed, agitated) you believe in and adhere to and trust in and rely on God, believe and adhere to and trust in and rely also on me. In my Father's house there are many dwelling places (homes) if it were not so I would have told you, for I'm going away to prepare a place for you. And when I go and make ready a place for you, I will come back again and will take you to myself, that where I am you may be also. And since we have such a great, and wonderful, and noble priest; who rules over the house of God, let us all come forward and draw near with true (honest and sincere) hearts in unqualified assurance and absolute conviction engendered by faith by that learning of the entire human personality on God in absolute trust and confidence in his power, wisdom, and goodness. Having our hearts sprinkled and purified from a guilty (evil) conscience and our bodies cleansed with pure water. So let us seized and hold fast and retain without wavering the hope we cherish and confess and our acknowledgement of it, for he who promised is reliable (sure) and faithful to his word. And when he has said this, even as they were looking at him, he was caught up, and a cloud received and carried him away out of their sight. And while they were gazing intently into heaven as he went, be-hold two men dressed in white robes suddenly stood beside them.

Who said men of Galilee, and why do you stand gazing into heaven? This same Jesus, who was caught away and lifted up from among you into heaven, will returned in just the same way in which you saw him go into heaven. Then the disciples went back to Jerusalem from the hill called Olivet which is near Jerusalem, only a Sabbath day's journey three quarters of mile away.

Jesus Rose from the Dead for Us

Chapter Seventeen

The Resurrection of the Dead and the Final Judgment.

I declare to you brothers, that flesh and blood cannot inherit the kingdom of God, nor does the perishable inherit the imperishable. Listen, I tell you a mystery. We will not all sleep means that Christians alive at that day will not have to died, but will be transformed immediately. A trumpet blast will usher in the new heaven and earth in a flash, in the twinkling of an eye, at the last trumpet, for the trumpet will sound, the dead will be raised imperishable and we will be change. The Jesus would understand the significance of this because trumpets were always blown to signal the start of great festivals and other extraordinary events. (I Corinthians Chapter 15:52-58) For the perishable must clothe itself with the imperishable, and the mortal with Immortality, when the perishable has been clothed with the imperishable, and the mortal with immortality, then the saying that is written will come true. Death has been swallowed up in victory. Where death is your victory? Where O death is your sting of death is sin, and the power of sin is the Law. But thanks be to God, he give us victory through our Lord Jesus Christ. Satan seemed to be victorious in the Garden of Eden and at the cross of Jesus, but Christ rose from death. Jesus Christ won the victory when he resurrected from his death. Christ Jesus overcame it, one day or hope over or beyond grave. However, my dear brothers stand firm, let nothing move you. Always give yourself fully to the work of the Lord, because you know your labor in the Lord is not in vain.

The Resurrection of the Dead and the Final Judgment.

GOD RAISED YOU UP TOGETHER WITH JESUS

Jesus death was for you, so was his resurrection. As for you were dead in your transgressions and sins, in which you used to live when you followed the ways of this world and of the ruler of the kingdom of the air. Because of his great love for us, God, who is rich in Mercy, made us alive with Christ even when we were dead in transgressions. It is by grace you have been saved. And God raised us up with Christ and seated us with him in the heavenly realms in Christ Jesus. (Ephesians 2:1-6 Colossians 3:1-3)

He raised you up together with Jesus to give you knew life. God has saved us and called us to a holy life not be-cause of anything we have done but because of his own purpose and grace. This grace was given us in Christ Jesus before the beginning of this world or time but it has now been revealed through the appearing of our savior Christ Jesus who has destroyed death and has brought life and Immortality to light through gospel. Jesus rose up together with us to give a new birth. Praised be to the God and Father of our Lord Jesus Christ in his great mercy.
He has given us a new birth into a living hope through the resurrection of Jesus Christ from the dead. Therefore, if anyone is in Christ, he is a new creature, the old has gone the new has come.

God raised him up to give you victory over Satan. Little children, you are of God and have defeated and overcome them because he who lives in you is greater than he who is in the world. No weapon fashion against you shall prosper, and every tongue that shall rise against you in Judgment, you shall condemn for this is the heritage of the servant of the Lord for his righteousness is of me; says the Lord Jesus of Host. After his death on the cross Jesus lay in the grave for three days then God raised his son from the dead (Read Matthew 28) And who through the spirit of holiness was declared with power to be the son of God by his resurrection from the dead Jesus Christ our Lord (Romans 1:14)

REWARDS OR JUDGEMENT

The Lord told us, take no thoughts, saying, what shall we eat or, what shall we drink? Or how we are clothed? Your heavenly Father knows that you have needs of all these things, but seek ye first the kingdom of God and his righteousness, and all these things shall be added unto you (Matthew 6:31-33)

The Judgment Throne of Christ

For we must all appear before the judgment seat of Christ, that every one may receive the things done in his body, according to that he hath done, whether it be good or bad (2 Corinthians 5:10) The Greek word for Judgment Seat is bema, which means "raised platform". It is not a judge's Bench, where a stern jurist sits and decides what kind of punishment to give each defendant. The Bema was more like a raised platform, or reviewing stand, where the judges of the contest or the race decide which Rewards to give to each contestant or runner.

Christ will sit at that bema or reviewing stand, if after being born again (John 3:3) we live a life of faithful service to the Lord, a life rich in good works, Christ will reward us at His Judgment Throne. At the judgment seat of Christ, we will be rewarded or our works will burn as hay and may have a little or no reward. Now if any man build upon this foundation gold, silver, precious stones, wood, hay, stubble, Every man's work shall be made manifest: for the day shall it, because it shall be revealed by fire; and the fire shall try every man's work of what sort it is.If any man's work shall be burned, shall suffer loss: but he shall be saved; yet so as by fire. (1 Corinthians 3: 10-15). If any man's work abide Apostle Paul said," He shall receive a reward".

REWARDED FOR FAITHFUL SERVICE

God will bless those who lay down their lives for Jesus to save others. He will graciously provide and take care of his servants. But God has not called us to go where there is the most gold. He has called us to go where the Holy Spirit might lead us. It may be a hard people as was Jeremiah's call (Jeremiah 6:9) hear, O earth, behold I will bring evil upon this people even the fruits of their thoughts, because they have not hearkened unto my words, nor to my law, but rejected it.

JUDGE FOR UNFAITHFULNESS

Not everyone who say to me Lord, Lord, will enter the kingdom of heaven, but only he who does the will of my Father who is in heaven. Many will say to me on that day Lord, Lord, did we not prophesy in your name and in your name drive out demons and perform many miracles. Then, I will tell them plainly, I never knew you, away from me, you evil doers. (Mathew 7:21-23 NIV) your reward in heaven is based on what you have done for Christ on earth, and how, (with what motive) you did it. To use Christ power to heal, to cast out devils and prophesy while living in the fleshly defilements of loving money, loving the praise of men and loving in immortality will bring divine judgment. What is that Judgment?

THE RESURRECTION OF THE DEAD AND FINAL JUDGMENT

I declare to you, brothers, that flesh and blood cannot inherit the Kingdom of God, nor does the perishable inherit the imperishable. Listen, I tell you a Mystery, we will not all sleep, but we will all be changed. We will not all sleep means that Christians alive at that day will not have to die but will be transformed immediately. A trumpet blast will usher in the New Heaven and Earth. In a flash, in the twinkling of an eye, at the last trumpet, for the trumpet will sound, the dead will be raised imperishable and we will be changed. The Jesus would understand the significance of this because trumpets were always blown to signal the start of great festivals and other extraordinary events.

(I Corinthians 15:54 - 57) For the perishable must clothe itself with the imperishable, and the mortal with the immortality. When the perishable has been clothed with the imperishable, and the mortal with the immortality, then the saying that are written will come true. Death has been swallowed up in victory. Where death is your victory? Where death is your sting? The sting of death is sin, and the Power of Sin is the Law. But thanks be to God, He gives us victory through Our Lord Jesus Christ. Satan seemed to be victorious in the Garden of Eden and at the Cross of Jesus. But God turned Satan's apparent victory into defeat when Jesus Christ rose from death. Jesus Christ won the victory when he resurrected from death. Jesus Christ won the victory when he resurrected from his death. Christ Jesus overcame it, one day we Christians will likewise gain victory over death or hope over or be-yond grave. Therefore my dear brother's stand grim, let nothing move you. Always give yourself fully to the work of the Lord, because you know your labor in the Lord is not in vain.

Rewards or Judgment

The Lord told us, take no thought, saying what shall we eat of what shall we drink? Or how shall we be clothed? You heavenly father knows that you have need of all these things. But seek ye first the Kingdom of God and the righteousness and all these things shall be added unto you. (Matthew 6:31-33)

Reward for Faithful Service

God will bless those who lay down their lives for Jesus to serve others. He will graciously provide and take care of His servants. But God has not called us to go where there is the most gold. He has called us to go where the Holy Spirit might lead us. It may be a hard people as was Jeremiah's call. (Jeremiah 6:9) Hear, O' Earth, behold I will bring evil upon this people even the fruit of their thoughts, because they have not hearkened unto my words, nor to my law, but rejected it.

Judged For Unfaithfulness

Not everyone who say to me Lord, Lord will enter the Kingdom of Heaven, but only he who does the will of my father who is in heaven. Many will say to me on that day Lord, Lord, did we not prophesy in your name, and in your name drive out demons and perform many miracles? Then I will tell them plainly, I never knew you, Away from me, you evildoers. (Matthew 7:21-23 NIV)

Your reward in heaven is based on what you have done for Christ on Earth, and how (with what motive) you did it. To use Christ power to heal, to cast out devils and prophesy while living in the fleshly defilements of loving money, loving the praise of men and loving in immorality will bring divine judgment. What is that Judgment? The judgment on this group of Christian ministers was this depart from me.

The Second Coming of Jesus Christ

Whenever you eat this bread and drink this cup, you have proclaimed the Lord's death until He comes. (Corinthians 11:26) Therefore, whosoever shall eat this bread and drink this cup of the Lord, unworthily, shall be guilty of the body and blood of the Lord. What Christ Jesus revealed through his servant Apostle Paul to us was that whenever we come together to dine or commune with him to eat the bread which is His body that was broken for us and the drink which also stand for the blood of the Lord Jesus which was shed on our behalf for the forgiveness of sin, then anytime we eat and drink, from the Lord's table we should proclaim the Lord's death until He comes, that is to say we must tell others about Christ Jesus, His work here on Earth, He was crucified and died on the cross without a cause, He was sinless. He was buried after His death, three days after his burial Jesus resurrected from death, He was ascended into heaven and He will come again to judge every person according to his good work or his bad works. "For we must all appear before the Judgment seat of Christ that every one may receive the things done in his body, according to that he hath done, whether it be good or bad. (2 Corinthians 5:10)

Jesus spoke about His own return immediately after the tribulation of those days shall the sun be darkened, and the moon shall not give her light, and the stars shall fall from heaven, and the powers of the heavens shall be shaken. And then shall appear the sign of the son of man in heaven and then shall all tribes of the Earth mourn, and they shall see the son of man coming in the clouds of Heaven with power and great glory. And He shall send His angels with a great sound of a trumpet and they shall gather together his elect from the four winds, from one end of heaven to the other.

From the fig tree, learn this lesson: as soon as its young shoots becomes soft and ten-der and it puts out its leaves, you know of surety that the summer is near. So also when you see the signs, all taken together, coming to pass, you may know of a surety that Jesus is near, at the very doors. Jesus Christ gave us an illustration concerning his second coming, He used a fig tree as an example for us to learn, there are three sea-sons in every year, Spring, Winter Summer and all are very important in our lives. During the spring time, fig tree put off its leaves to soon as young shoots becomes soft and tenders that, is to say the old leaves will begin to drop down one by one, one will see or know that all the leaves on the tree had fallen down remaining the branches alone, then new leaves will begin to shoot up, Jesus Our King told us to be watchful about when the leaves started to drop form the tree it tell us that Summertime is very close, or near, likewise also when we see these signs taken place or coming to pass we supposed to know that his second coming is right at the door., What are the signs of his coming?

Many will come in my name saying "I am the Christ the Messiah" and they will lead many astray. Jesus told us to be very careful so that no one misleads you. This prophecy has come to pass, many deceivers are out to lead you to a wrong place so you must be careful all the time. Matt 24:6 And you will hear wars, see that you are not frightened or troubled, for this must take place, but the end is not yet. For nation will rise up against nation and kingdom against kingdom and there will be famines and earthquakes in places after places. Our King and Lord for telling His people these things over two thousand years ago and it has completely fulfilled Nation warning against Nations and Kingdom likewise. The love of most believers will grow cold but he that stands to the end shall be saved. And the Gospel of the Kingdom shall be preached to the whole world as a testimony after which the Son of Man shall come.

Forgiveness of Sin in the Place of His Second Coming

When Jesus was physically here on the Earth, His followers went to Him and asked Him to teach them how to pray as John the Baptizer thought his disciples to pray. According to Matthew Chapter 6 verses 12-15, Jesus thought them saying, And forgive us our debts as we also have forgiven (left, remitted and let of the debts, and have given up resentment against) our debtors. For if you forgive people their trespasses (their reckless sand willful sins, leaving them, letting them go, and giving up resentment) your heavenly Father will also forgive your trespasses. Moreover, if your brother sins against you, go and tell him his fault between you and him alone, if he hears you, you have gained your brother. But if he will not hear, take with you one or two more, that by the mouth of two or three witness every word may be established. And if he refuses to hear them, tell it to the church. But if he refuses even to hear the church, let him be to you like a heathen and a tax collector. The bible tells us that Joseph forgave his brothers who sold him to slavery. Joseph reassures his brothers when his brothers saw that their father was dead, they said perhaps Joseph will hate us and may actually repay us for all the evil which we did to him. So they sent us messengers to Joseph saying "Before your father died he commanded saying. Thus you shall say to Joseph, I beg you, please forgive the trespasses of your brothers and their sin, for they did evil to you." Now please forgive the trespass of the servants, of the God your father. And Joseph wept when they spoke to him. Then his brothers also wept when they spoke to him. Then his brothers also went and fall down before his face, and they said, behold, we are your servants. Joseph said to them, do not be afraid, for am I in the place of God? But as for you, you meant evil against me, but God meant it for good, in order to bring it about as it is this day to save many people alive. I John 1:9 the word of God says if we confess our sins, He is faithful and just to forgive us our sins and to cleanse us from all unrighteousness. Peter came up to Him and said, Lord, how many times may my brother sin against me and I forgive him and let it go? As many as up to seven times? Jesus answered him, I tell you, not up to seven times, but seventy times seven.

  Therefore, the Kingdom of Heaven is like a human kingdom who wish to settle accounts with his attendants. When he began the accounting, one was brought to him who owed him 10,000 talents. (Probably $10,000) And because he could not pay his master ordered him to be sold, with his wife and his children and everything that he possessed, and payment to be made. So the attendant fell on his knees, begging him have patience with me and I will pay you everything. And his master's heart was moved with compassion, and he released him and forgave him. Cancelling the debt. But the same attendant, as he went out, found one of his fellow attendants, who owed him one hundred denarii (about twenty dollars) and he caught him by the throat and said, pay what you owe, so his fellow attendant fell down and begged him earnestly, give me time, and I will pay you all, but was unwilling and he went out and had him put in prison till he should pay the debt. When his fellow attendants saw what had happened, they were greatly distressed, and they went and told everything that had taken place to their master. Then his master called him and said to him, you contemptible and wicked attendant, I forgive and cancelled all that (great) debt of yours because you begged me to. And should you not have had pity and mercy on your fellow attendant, as I had pity and mercy on you? And in wrath his master turned him over to the torturers (Jailers) till he should pay all that he owed.

So also my heavenly Father will deal with every one of you, if you do not freely forgive your brother from your heart his offences. Jesus told His followers in the Book of Mark. Chapter 11:24-26 For this reason I am telling you, whatever you ask for in prayer, believe, trust and be confident that it is granted to you, and you will get it. And whenever you stand praying, if you have anything against anyone, forgive him and let it drop, leave it, let it go. In order that your Father who is in heaven may also forgive you your own failings and shortcomings and let them drop. But if you do not forgive, neither will your Father in heaven forgive your failings and shortcomings. Jesus said in Luke 13:3-4 Take heed to your selves, if your brother sins against you, rebuke him, and if he repents, forgive him. And if he sin against you seven times in a day, and seven times in a day returns to you, saying, I repent, you shall forgive him. Unforgiving Spirit can be a hindrance to your prayers, so we must learn how to forgive one another.

Brethren, any gift given to us by God, we will surely give an account of it to God who give to us, he who, that more is given to, more is also expected from him, whatever talents that God has given to us, we should use it wisely. Jesus to his disciples the parable of the wise and foolish virgins. In the book of Matthew chapter 25:1-13 Then the Kingdom of Heaven shall be likened to ten virgins who took their lamps and took no oil with them, but the wise took oil in their vessels with their lamps. But while the bridegroom delayed of coming, they all fell asleep and at midnight there was a cry made behold the bridegroom cometh, go out to meet him. Then all the virgins arouse and trimmed their lamps. And the foolish said to the wise, give us some of your oil, for our lamps are going out. But the wise answered, saying, No, lest there should not be enough for us and you, but go rather to those who sell, and buy for yourselves. And while they went to buy, the bridegroom came, and those who were ready went in with him to the wedding, and the door was shut. Afterward, the other virgins came also, saying, Lord, Lord, open to us, but he answered and said, Assuredly, I say to you, I do not know you. Watch therefore, for you know neither the day nor the hour in which the Son of Man is coming.

Our Lord and Savior, Jesus Christ, here is giving us a clear picture to prepare while waiting for His Second Coming, he is telling us to be as wise as the five who took extra oil in their vessels. We are Christ Ambassador, bride, we are now engaged to Christ, He is the bridegroom, we are waiting here on Earth until we will be taken to heaven, to the marriage

The Resurrection of the Dead and the Final Judgment.

ceremony where we believers will be wedded to Christ Jesus Our Lord. And do this, knowing the time that now it is high time to awake up out of sleeping, for now our salvation is nearer than when we first believed. The night is far spent, the day is at hand, therefore let us cast off the works of darkness, and let us put on the armor of light. Let us walk properly, as in the day not in revelry and drunkenness, not in lewdness and lust, not in strife and envy. But put on the Lord Jesus Christ make no provision for the flesh to fulfill its lusts.

Chapter Eighteen

What Is Faithfulness In Service?

For the Kingdom of heaven is like a man traveling to a far country, who called his own servants and delivered his goods to them. And to one he gave five talents, to another two, and to another one, to each according to his own ability, and immediately he went and traded with them, and made another five talents. And likewise, he who has received two gained two more also. But he who had received one went and dug in the ground, and hid his Lord's money. Believers, or the Saints, or the children of God, we are the servants, that the master gave to us his talents, some five, some two and some also one talent. God has given to us different kinds of gifts. Deuteronomy 7:9 Tell us that know, recognize, and understand therefore that the Lord your God, He is God, the Faithful God, who keeps covenant and steadfast love and mercy with those who love Him and keep His commandments, to a thousand generations. The God who has called us unto himself is a faithful God that made a covenant with Abraham, saying and I will establish my covenant between me and you and your descendants after you and their generations, for an everlasting covenant, and I will be God to you and your descendants after you. Also I give to you and your descendants after you the land in which you are a stranger, all the land of Canaan, as an everlasting possession and I will be their God. Because of the faithfulness of God he was able to bring to pass when he told Abraham that your descendant will go to slavery for four hundred years after that I will free them from the house of slavery and bring them to the land which I promised you, the land of the Canaan which you are a stranger today.

Joseph was sold in to the land of Egypt, his brothers hated him the more and sold him to slavery. Joseph became a prisoner in the land of Egypt when his master's wife wanted to sleep with him, he refused to do that because he doesn't want to sin against God and his master, the wife of his master lied against him which led him in prison, God promoted him when Pharaoh dreamed God gave him the Interpretation so he became second to Pharaoh. Through Joseph, his father and his brethren came to Egypt, after the death of Joseph, Israelites were in great problem because they were treated as slaves in Egypt. When the appointed time that God told Abraham has reached they cried to God and he delivered them through his servant Moses and led them to the Promised land.

Psalm 89:34 God said through his servant, David My Covenant will I not break or profane, nor after the thing that is gone out of my lips. Blessed be the Lord, who has given rest to his people Israel, according to all he promised. There has not failed one word of all his good promise, which he promised through His servant Moses.

Jesus approaching and breaking silence, said to them, all authority all power of ruling in heaven and on earth has been given to me. Jesus Christ was faithful when he was physically here on earth, the bible tells me that there was no sin found in him when he lived thirty-three years here on earth. Jesus said my food is to do the will of him, who sent me and to finish his work. Go therefore and make disciples of all the nations, baptizing them in the name of the Father, and of the Son and of the Holy Spirit, teaching them to observe all things that I have commanded you and I am with you always, even to the end of the age- Amen. Our Lord Jesus came to seek and to save the lost. And they that are wise shall shine as the brightness of the firmament, and they that turn many to righteousness as the stars forever and ever. When the Lord Jesus resurrected from death he came to his followers and gave them this Commandments to go and preach the word of God to the lost sinner, to repent and accept him as their Lord and Personal Savior. Mark 15:15-18 also tell us the same but only faithful people will obey this saying or commandments.

Jesus instructed us to occupy till he comes. When the master was travelling he gave talents to his servants. He gave five talents to one of his servant and he worked hard and have five more talent which mean he got profit of five making ten talent and the other who got two talents went and worked hard and got two more profit, this shows that they were faithful and obedient to their Master, Hannah proved herself faithful in the service of God, when she need a child, Then Elkanah her husband said to her, Hannah, why do you cry? And why do you not eat? And why are you grieving? Am I not more to you than ten sons? So Hannah rose after they have eaten drunk in Shiloh. Now Eli the Priest was sitting on the seat beside a post of the temple (tent) of the Lord. And Hannah was in distress of soul, praying to the Lord and weeping bitterly. She vowed, saying O Lord of hosts, if you will indeed look on the affliction of your handmaid but will give me a son, I will give him to the Lord all his life, no razor shall touch his head. And Elkanah knew Hannah his wife, and the Lord remembered her so it came to pass in the process of time that Hannah conceived and bore a son, called his name Samuel saying because I have asked him from the Lord. Now when she had weaned him, she took him up with her, with three bulls, one Ephah of flour, and a skin of wine, and brought him to the house of the Lord in Shiloh. And the child was young. Then they slaughter a bull and brought the child to Eli. Hannah vowed to the Lord and she was faithful to God and fulfilled her promise by giving her son Samuel to God all the days of her life and God bless Samuel and He became a great judge and prophet in Israel.

The Results of Faithful Men in Service

In the household of God we need faithful men and women, those who could be trusted, in our working place and also our families we need people who could be trusted, when electing a president we need to elect a faithful person. Joseph found favor in the sight of his master and served him, and all the works of his master did prosper in his hand so his master handed everything in his house in the care of Joseph and through Joseph the Lord blessed Potiphar, and officer to Pharaoh. The bible says in Genesis 39:9 So Joseph said, there is no one greater in this house than I nor has he kept back anything from me but you, because you are his wife. How can I do this great wickedness, and sin against God? There was a man in the Bible days that God found him very faithful and his name was Job, he was very, rich yet respectful and fearful to God, he was blameless and upright, and one who fear God and shunned evil. And seven sons and three daughters was born to him, seven thousand sheep, three thousand camels, five hundred of ox, five hundred donkeys, God himself testified about this man when the Lord said to Satan from where do you come? So Satan answered the Lord and said from going to and fro on the earth, and from walking back and forth on it. Then the Lord said to Satan from where do you come? So Satan answered the Lord and said from going to and fro on the earth, and from walking back and forth on it. Then the Lord said to Satan, have you considered my servant Job, that there is none like him on the earth. Satan attacked Job and he lost all his possessions just one day including his children, then his wife told him to curse God and die do you still hold to your faith and integrity. But Job said to her, you speak as one of the foolish women speaks. Shall we indeed accept well from God and shall not accept adversity? In all this Job did not sin with his lips. The end results of Job was better than his beginning. And the Lord restored Job loses when he prayed for his friends, indeed the Lord gave Job twice as much as he had before. Daniel was another man of God who was faithful in the service of God, then Daniel distinguished himself above the governors, because an excellent spirit was within him, and the King gave thought to set him over the whole realm.

The True Bride of Christ

And these came unto me one of the seven angels which had the seven vials full of the seven plagues, and talked with me saying come hither, I will show thee the bride, the Lamb's wife, and he carried me away in the Spirit to a great and high mountain, and showed me that great city, the New Jerusalem, descending out of heaven from God. Having the Glory of God and her light was like unto a stone most precious even like a Jasper stone, clear as crystal.

The word bride is used only five times in connection with believers. In John Gospel 3:29 He who has the bride is the bridegroom, but the friend of the bridegroom, who stands and hears him, rejoices greatly because of the bridegroom's voice. Therefore this joy of mine is fulfilled. Revelation 21:2 also says Then I John saw the holy city, New Jerusalem, coming down, out of heaven from God, prepared as a bride adorned for her husband. Thirdly from Revelation 21:9 Then one of the seven angels who had the seven bowls filled with the seven last plagues came to me and talked with me, saying, come I will show you the bride, the Lamb's wife. Revelation 22:17 and the Spirit and the bride say, come! And let him who hears say, come! And let him who thirsts come. Whoever desires, let him take the water of life freely. Matthew 9:15 And Jesus said to them, can the friends of the bridegroom mourn as long as the bridegroom is with them? But the days will come when the bridegroom will be taken away from them, and then they will fast. The bride of Christ is not the Israel of the Old Testament times 2. It is not part of the New Testament Church. It is not the whole of the New Testament Church. It is not the one forty four thousand Jews. It is not the tribulation saints. It is not any single individual or any one special group of denomination or all denomination combined. What the bride of Christ is- It is that great city, holy Jerusalem (Rev 21;2,9-10) This is what the angel pointed out to John when he promised to show him that bride, the Lamb's wife, the Holy City, the heavenly Jerusalem. There it is unscriptural to speak of any one company of redeemed as being the exclusive bride of Christ Jesus. If the city the New Jerusalem is the bride then all who go to live in the Holy City make up the bride and not just part of them.

All the redeemed saint will live in the city. The Old Testament saints were promised the New Jerusalem according to the Hebrews. 11:10-16 for he waited for a city which has foundations, whose builder and maker is God. By faith, Sarah herself has received strength to conceive seed, and she bore a child when she was past the age, because she judged Him faithful who had promised. Therefore from one man and him as good as dead were born as many as the stars of the sky in the multitude. Innumerable as the sand which is by the seashore. These all died in faith not having received the promises but having seen them afar off were assured of them, embraced them and confessed that they were strangers and pilgrims on the Earth. For those who say such things declare plainly that they seek a homeland. And truly if they had called to mind that country from which they had come out, they would have had opportunity to return. But now they desire a better that is heavenly country. Therefore God is not ashamed to be called their God, for He has prepared a city for them.

The Earthly Church Was Promised the City

According to the Gospel of (John Chapter 14:1-3) Do not let your hearts be troubled, distressed, agitated. You believe in and adhere to and trust in and rely on God, believe in and adhere to and trust in and rely also on me. In my Father's house, there are many dwelling places, (homes) if it were not so, I would have told you, for I am going away to prepare a place for you. And when if I go and make ready a place for you, I will come back again and will take you to myself, that where I am you may be also. Jesus Christ the Son of the Most High God when he was physically here on the earth gave this important promise to the church that he would go back to His heavenly Father, to prepare a place for His people. Hebrew 13:14 says, for here we have no continuing city, but we seek the one to come.

Every Christian is promised the city, He who overcomes, I will make him a pillar in the temple of My God, and he shall go out no more. I will write on him the name of My God and the name of the New Jerusalem, which comes down out of Heaven from My God. And I will write on him a new name. Revelation 3:12 John 14:1-3 He-brew 12:22-22 But you have come to Mount Zion and to the city of the Living God, the heavenly Jerusalem, to an innumerable company of angels, to the general Assembly and church of the first born who are registered in heaven, to God the Judge of all, to the spirits of just men made perfect. The one hundred and forty four thousand saints of the Jew were promised to be in the city of Jerusalem in heaven. The tribulation saints will go there. The bible says in the book of Revelation 6:9-11 when he opened the fifth seal, I saw under the altar the souls who had been slain for the Word of God and for the testimony which they held. And they cried with a loud voice, saying, How long, O Lord, holy and true, until you judge and avenge our blood and those who dell on the earth? Then a white robe was given to each of them, and it was said to them that they should rest a little while longer, until both the number of their fellow servants and their brethren, who would be killed as they were, was completed. A multitude of people from the Great Tribulation- After these things I looked, and behold, a great multitude which no one could number, of all nations, tribes, peoples and tongues, standing before the throne and before the Lamb, clothed with white robes, with palm branches in their hands, and crying out with a loud voice, saying, salvation belongs to our God who sits on the throne, and the Lamb. All the angels stood around the throne, and the Lamb. All the angels stood around the throne and the elders and the four living creatures, fell on their faces before the throne and worshipped God, saying, Amen, Blessing and glory and wisdom, Thanksgiving and honor and power and might be to our God forever and ever, Amen. The book of Revelation 15:2-4 says, And I saw something like a sea of glass mingled with fire, and those who have the victory over the beast, over his image and over his mark and over the number of his name, standing on the sea of glass, having harps of God. They sing the song of Moses, the servant of God, and the Song of the Lamb, saying, great and marvelous are your works, Lord God Almighty. Just and true are your ways, King of the Saints, who shall not fear you, O Lord, and glorify your name? For you alone are holy.

For all nations shall come and worship before you. For your judgments have been manifested. The Saints reign with Christ for one thousand years. And I saw thrones, and they that sat on them, and judgment was committed to them. Then I saw the souls of those who had been beheaded for their witness to Jesus and for the word of God, who had not worshipped the beast or his image, and had not received his mark on their foreheads or on their hands. And they lived and reigned with Christ for a thousand years. But the rest of the dead did not live again until the thousand years were finished. This is the first resurrection. Blessed and holy is he who has part in the first resurrection. Over such the second death has no power, but they shall be priests of God and of Christ, and shall reign with him a thousand years. Therefore we conclude that since all saints in the first resurrection from Abel to the last one saved in the future tribulation will go to live in the New Jerusalem that all such saints will be members of the bride, no one person, group of persons, denomination, mansion, temple or any other building can be called the City Lamb's wife. It is scriptural however to say concerning the redeemed, that they are now married to Christ under the terms of the New Covenant that they are citizens of heaven, that they have hope of going to live in the New Jerusalem, and because of this they expect to be a part of the bride of Christ or part of the heavenly City. But no one is actually a part of the bride until he begins to live in that beautiful city of New Jerusalem which is the bride, the Lamb's wife. (Revelation 21:9-10).

  The church who is the bride of Christ is now married. Jesus called himself the bridegroom of Christians. And Jesus said to them, Can the friends of the bridegroom mourn as long as the bridegroom is with them? But the days will come when the bridegroom will be taken away from them, and then they will fast. The Disciples of John the Baptist came to Jesus to ask him questions, saying, why do we and the Pharisees fast often, but your disciples do not fast, Jesus answered them that as far as the bridegroom is with the bride, they could not fast but when the bridegroom is taken away from them then the bride and her friends will fast. When Jesus Christ after his death and resurrection, he was ascended into heaven, then the disciples of the Lord Jesus also fasted. When a bridegroom wedded to her bride and they went to the honey moon, they cannot go there and start fasting while people are there to serve them. John the Baptist called Jesus Christ the bridegroom. John 3:29 He who has the bride is the bridegroom, but the friend of the bridegroom, who stands and hears him, rejoices greatly because of the bridegroom's voice. Therefore, this joy of mine is fulfilled. Christians are married to God and Christ under terms of the New Testament and the Israel was married to God under the terms of the Old Testament Matthew 26:26-30.

And as they were eating, Jesus took the bread, blessed and broke it and gave it to the disciples and said, Take, eat, this is my body. Then He took the cup, drink from it all of you. For this is my blood of the New Covenant which is shed for many for the remission of sins. But I say to you, I will not drink of this fruit of the vine from now on until that day when I drink it new with you in my Father's Kingdom, and when they had sung a hymn, they went out to the Mount Olives.

Jesus Christ the Mediator of the New Covenant, and to the blood of sprinkling that speaks better things than the blood of Abel. Apostle Paul taught Christians are married to Christ Jesus by the New Covenant, see Romans 7:1-6 or do you not know, brethren for I speak to those who know the Law, that the law has dominion over a man as long as he lives? For the woman who has a husband is bound by the law to her husband as long as he lives. But if the husband dies, she is released from the law of her husband. So then, if while her husband lives, she marries another man, she will be called adulteress, but if the husband dies, she is free from the law, so that she is no adulteress, though she has married another man. Therefore, my brethren, you also have become dead to the law through the body of Christ, that you may be married to another to Him who was raised from the dead, that you should bear the fruit to God. For when we were in the flesh, the sinful passions which were aroused by the law were at work in our members to bear fruits to death. But now we have been delivered from the law, having died to what we were held by, so that we should serve in the newness of the Spirit and not in the oldness of the letter. Jesus revealed to us in Revelation 22:16-17 That I, Jesus, have sent my Messenger (angel) to you to witness and give you assurance of these things for the Churches (assemblies) I am the Root (the source) and the offspring of David, the radiant and brilliant morning star. The Holy Spirit and the bride of the Christ, the true Christians says come. And let him who is listening say come. And let everyone come who is thirsty, (who is painfully conscious of his need of those things by which the soul is refreshed, supported and strengthened and whoever desires to do it, let him come, take, appropriate and drink water of life without cost. (Isaiah 55:1) This is an invitation to abundant life. Ho! Everyone who thirsts, come to the waters, and you who have no money, come, buy and eat. Yes, come buy wine and milk without money and without price. And he said to me, it is done, I am the Alpha and Omega, the Beginning and the End. I will give of the fountain of the water of life freely to him who thirsts. He who overcomes shall inherit all things, and I will be his God and he shall be my son. The bible says in Isaiah 61:10 I will greatly rejoice in the Lord, my Soul shall be joyful in my God, for he has clothed me with the garments of salvation. He has covered me with the robe of righteousness, as a bridegroom decks himself with jewels. Revelation 19:14-15 and the troops of heaven, clothed in fine linen, dazzling and clean, followed Him on white horses. Jude 1:14-15 Now Enoch, the seventh from Adam, prophesized about these men also, saying, behold the Lord comes with ten thousands of His saints. To execute judgment on all, to convict all who are ungodly among them of all their ungodly among them of all their ungodly deeds which they have committed in an ungodly way, and of all the harsh things which ungodly sinners have spoken against Him.

Daniel 7:9 I watched till thrones were put in place, and the Ancient of Days was seated. His garment was as white as snow. And the hail of His head was like pure wool. His throne was a fiery flame, its wheels a burning fire. A fiery stream issued and came forth from before Him. A thousand thousands ministered to Him, ten thousand times ten thousand stood before Him. The court was seated and the books were opened.

The Revelation of Jesus Christ, which God gave Him to show His servants things which must shortly take place? And he sent and signified it by His angels to His Servant John, who bore witness to the Word of God, and to the testimony of Jesus Christ, to all things that he saw. Blessed is he who reads and those who hear the Words of this prophecy, and keep those things which are written in it for the time is near.

Grace to you and peace to Him, who is and who was and who is to come and from the seven spirits who are before His throne, and from Jesus Christ the faithful witness, the first born from the dead, and the ruler over the Kings of the earth. To whom who loved us and washed us from our sins in His own blood. Read Psalm 89:27-29 Says, also I will make Him my first born, the highest of the Kings of the earth. My Mercy, I will not keep from Him forever and My Covenant shall stand firm with him. His seed also I will make to endure forever. And His throne as the days of heaven. And has made us Kings and Priests to his God and Father, to him be glory and dominion forever and ever- Amen.
Behold, He is coming with clouds, and every eye will see Him, even they who pierced Him. And all tribes of the Earth will mourn, because of Him, even so Amen. I am the Alpha and the Omega, the Beginning and the End says the Lord, who is and who was and who is to come, the Almighty.

I, John, your brother and companion in the tribulation and the Kingdom and patience of Jesus Christ, was on the Island that is called Patmos for the word of God and the testimony of Jesus Christ. I was in the spirit on the Lord's day, and I heard behind me a loud voice, as a trumpet, saying, I am the Alpha and the Omega, the First and the Last, and what you see, write in the book and send it to the Seven Churches which are Asia, to Ephesus, to Smyrna, to Pergamos, to Thyatira, Sardis, to Philadelphia and to Laodicea. Then John turned to see the voice that spoke with him. And having turned I saw the seven golden lampstands and in the midst of the seven lampstands one like the Son of Man, clothed with a garment down to the feet and girded about the chest with a golden band. His head and hair were white like a wool, as white as snow, and His eye like a flame of fire. (Daniel 7:13-14) says I saw in the night visions and behold, on the clouds of the heavens came one like a son of man, and He came to the Ancient of Days and was presented before Him. And there was given Him (the Messiah) dominion and glory kingdom that all peoples, nations and languages should serve Him. His dominion is an everlasting dominion which shall not pass away, and His Kingdom is one of which shall not be destroyed.

The book of Revelation Chapter 5:1-10 confirmed what Daniel saw. And I saw in the right hand of Him who sat on the throne a scroll written inside and on the back, sealed with seven seals. Then I saw a strong angel proclaiming with loud voice, who is worth to open the scroll and to lose its seals? And no one in heaven or on the earth or under the earth was able to open the scroll, or to look at it, so I wept much, because no one was found worthy to open and read the scroll, or look at it. But one of the elders said to me. Do not weep. Behold, the Lion of the tribe of Judah, the Root of David has prevailed to open the scroll and lose its seven seals. And I looked, and behold, in the midst of the throne and the four living creatures, and in the midst of the elders, stood a Lamb as though it had been slain, having seven horns and seven eyes, which the seven Spirits of God are sent out in all the earth. Then He came and took the scroll out of the right hand of Him who sat on the throne. Now when He had taken the scroll, the four living creatures and the twenty four elders fell down before the Lamb, each having a

harp, and golden bowls full of Incense, which are the prayers of the saints. And they sang a new song, saying, you are worthy to take the scroll. And to open its seals, for you were slain, and have redeemed us to God by your blood out of every tribe and tongue and people and nation, and have made us Kings and Priests to our God, and we shall reign on the earth. Daniel 10:5 says I lifted my eyes and looked, and behold a man clothed in linen, whose loins were girded with pure gold of phase.
In Revelation Chapter 1:14 John saw His head and His hair were white like wool, as snow, and His eyes like a flame of fire.

His feet were like fine brass, as if refined in a furnace, and His voice as the sound of many waters. Daniel Chapter 10:6 says His body was like beryl, his face like the appearance of lightning, his eyes like touches of fire, his arms and feet like burnished bronze in color, and the sound of his words like the voice of multitude. In His right hand He held seven stars, and from His mouth there came forth a sharp two edged sword, and His face was like the sun shining in full power at midday. The book of Exodus 34:29-30 says when Moses came down from Sinai with the two tables of the Testimony in his hand, he did not know that the body of his skin of his face shone and sent forth beams by reason of his speaking with the Lord. And when Aaron and all the Israelites looked at Moses and saw his face shining, they were afraid to come near him.

Chapter Nineteen

The Reasons Why One Hundred And Forty Four Thousand Are The Man Child.

It has been proven that the sun clothed woman is the national Israel. The man child then could not be either the Gentiles or the Church which is made up mainly of Gentiles. (Acts 15:13-18) And after they had become silent, James answered, saying, Men and brethren, listen to me, Simon he declared how God at the first visited the Gentiles to take out of them a people for His name. And with this the words of the prophets agree, just as it is written. After this I will return and will rebuild the tabernacle of David, which has fallen down, I will rebuild its ruins. And I will set it up, so that the rest of mankind may seek the Lord, says the Lord who does all these things. Known to God from eternity are all His works. The woman would have to produce of her own kind according to the Law of Reproduction given by God (Genesis chapter 1:22-28) Therefore if the woman is Jewish the man child must also be Jewish. The woman represent a company of people. There is no other company in the event of Revelation chapter 4-19 that could possibly be symbolized by the man child other than 144,000 Jews of Revelation chapter 7 and 14.

2. The man child cannot be Christ because everything from Revelation 4:1 on must be after the churches of Revelation 2:1 to Revelation 3:22 How could John see the historical ascension of Christ as happening among the things to be in the middle of Daniel's 70th week of 3 ½ years before the second advent of Christ.

3. The man child cannot be the Church as a whole, or in part, as some teach, because the church is raptured in Revelation 4:1

before the events of Revelation 4:22 which must be after the churches.

4. The man child represents a company of all living people who will be translated without seeing death, the woman brings forth either a dead or a living child, not one partly dead or not one partly alive, the dragon could not one already dead at birth (Rev 12:4) The child is caught up to God alive as soon as it is born (12:4-5) The 144,000 which must be after the churches, that could possibly be the man child whose life the dragon tries to take (Revelation 7:1-8, 14:1) Since the Old Testament Saints and the Church Saints are all resurrected to immortality by this time, it would be impossible for the dragon to kill them.

5. Revelation 7:1-8, 14:1-5, 9:4 give a complete revelation of the 144,000 their number, Salvation, sealing in the forehead, protection through the first six trumpets, rapture under the seven trumpet as the man child, and their destiny and position, in heaven after their rapture. If one of these passages is taken away the revelation about them is incomplete. We have them on earth all through the first six trumpets. Revelation 7:1-3, 9:4 and in heaven immediately after the catching up of the man child in the 7th trumpet. Revelation 14: 1-5 So if they are not the man child who is he and how did the 144,000 are before God's throne in heaven, having been redeemed from the earth and from among men. They are in heaven people that last 3 ½ years of tribulation is identical with that of the man child. (Revelation 12:5)

6. The time of the Rapture of the 144,000 proves them to be the man child. The time of their translation is identical with that of the man child. Revelation 12:5, 14:1-5

7. We have seen that the Church and the O.T. Saints are to be raptured before Daniel's 70th week and the tribulation. We have seen that the great multitude of tribulation Saints will be killed mainly after and raptured after the 144,000 in heaven (Revelation 6:9-11 7:9-17) The only other company caught up

beside these is the 144,000 and only place the rapture (Revelation 12:5) Therefore the man child and the 144,000 must be the same. If they are not the same, then we do not know whom the man child represents or how the 144,000 gets to heaven. Where is the revelation of their rapture if it is not in Revelation 12:5?

8. The place where the 144,000 saints are, in the book of Revelation 14:1-5 proves they will be in heaven during the last three and half years of the tribulation, so they must be raptured before then, when, if not as the man child? The Mount Zion is the heavenly one (see Hebrews, Chapter 12:22-24) But you have come to Mount Zion and to the City of the Living God, the heavenly Jerusalem, to an innumerable company of angels to the general assembly and Church of the firstborn who are registered in heaven, to God the Judge of all, to the Spirits of Just men made perfect, to Jesus the Mediator of the New Covenant, and to the blood of sprinkling that speaks better things than that of Abel. (Revelation 14:1-2) Then I looked, and behold the Lamb stood on Mount Zion, and with him 144,000 men who had His name and His Father's name inscribed on their foreheads. And I heard a voice from heaven like the sound of great waters and like the ramblings of mighty thunder, the voice I heard seemed like the music of harpist accompanying themselves on their harps.

9. The 144,000 are the first fruits to God from Israel after the rapture of every saved Jews and Gentiles of after the Church in Revelation 4:1 They are not saved when the Church is raptured or they would go up also, I Thessalonians 4:16 For the Lord Himself will descend from heaven with shout, with the voice of an archangel, and with the trumpet of God. And the dead in Christ will rise first. Then we who are alive and remain shall be caught up together with them in the cloud to meet the Lord in the air. And thus we shall always be with the Lord. But each in

his own rank and turn, Christ the Messiah is the first fruits, then those who are Christ's Own will be resurrected at His coming. (I Corinthians 15:23) Since they are saved after that in the first 3 ½ years of the tribulation, their tribulation must be the same as that of the man child, which represent a company of the Jews from Israel, were to be saved and raptured before the 144,000 then the man child will be first fruits to God from Israel and not the 144,000. But since the 144,000 are to be the first fruits, then it is clear that they are the first Jews saved and raptured from Israel during the tribulation of 7 years between the rapture of the Church and the Second Advent. This proves that the 144,000 are the ones symbolized by the man child.

There is only one company saved and raptured between the rapture of the church at the beginning of Daniel seventy week (70th week) and the rapture of the tribulation saints at the end of this week. The company is symbolized by the man child and clearly revealed to be 144,000 Jews (Revelation 7:1-8, 9:4, 12:5 Revelation 14:1-5) The 144,00 are specifically sealed for protection to go through the trumpet judgments only immediately after the seventh (7th) trumpet, which include all Revelation chapter 11:15 and 13:18 we see the 144,000 in heaven (Revelation 14:1-5) Then I looked, and behold, a lamb standing on Mount Zion, and with Him one hundred and forty-four thousand, having His father's name written on their foreheads.

> And I heard a voice of many waters, and like the voice of loud thunder. And I heard sound of harpists playing their harps. They sang as it were a new song before the throne, before the four living creatures, and before the elders, and no one could learn that song except the hundred and forty-four thousand who were redeemed from the Earth. These are the ones who were not defiled with women, for they are virgins. These are the ones who follow the Lamb wherever He goes. These were

redeemed from among men, being first fruits to God and to the Lamb. And in their mouth was found no deceit, for they are without fault before the Throne of God. They were spotless, untainted, without blemish, before the throne of God. The way God protects them from the wrath of Satan under the seventh (7th) trumpet is by catching them up to God and His throne. The woman, man child and remnant of the woman are the only Jewish Companies in the (Revelation chapter 12:1-2, 5 and 17) The 144,000 must be one of these three companies, for they are sealed out of all tribes of the Children of Israel (see Revelation 7:1-8) They are in no place mentioned separately from those three companies as a forth company and there is no indication of them as such, since they are one of the three companies, which one? They cannot be the woman or the remnant for these remain on Earth while the 144,000 are translated (Revelation 14:1-5)

The 144,000 therefore must be the man child. The 144,000 are the only one that could possibly fulfill the statement about man child in Revelation 12. The man child and the 144,000 represents a small company (Revelation 7:1-9) They both are caught up to God and throne (12:5) and Revelation 14:1-5 they both are delivered from the wrath of the dragon (Revelation 12:4-5) and they both are in heavenly people, so must be the same company. Prophet Isaiah chapter 66:7-8 says before she was in labor, she gave birth, before her pain came, and she delivered a male child. Who has heard such a thing? Who has seen such a thing? Shall the Earth be made to give birth in one day? Or Zion was in labor, she gave birth to her children. The Prophet predicts Israel as bringing forth the man child before she is delivered or saved at the end of the tribulation (Zachariah 12:10-14) And I will pour on the house of David and on the inhabitants of Jerusalem the spirit of grace

The Reasons Why One Hundred And Forty Four Thousand Are The Man Child.

and supplication, yes, they will mourn for Him as one mourns for his only son, and grave for Him as one grieves for a firstborn. In that day, there shall be a great mourning in Jerusalem, like the mourning at Hadad Rimmon in the pain of Megiddo. And the land shall mourn, every family by itself, and their wives by themselves, the family of the house of Levi by itself, and their wives by themselves, the family of Shimei by itself, and their wives by themselves. All the family that remain, every family by itself, and their wives by themselves. Romans 11:25-29 God, through Apostle Paul tells us that, For I do not desire, brethren, that you should be ignorant of this mystery, lest you be wise in your opinion, that blindness in part has happened to Israel until the fullness of the Gentiles has come in. And so all Israel will be saved, as it is written, The Deliverer will come out Zion, and He will turn away ungodliness from Jacob, for this is My Covenant with them, when I take away their sings. Concerning the gospel they are enemies for your sake, but concerning the election they are beloved for the sake of the fathers. For the gifts and the calling of God are irrevocable. Who is the man child that Israel is to bring forth before her own conversion at the Second Advent if not the 144,000 of Revelation 14:1-5, Revelation 7:1-8 and Daniel chapter 12:1

The Bible says, And at that time of the end Michael shall arise, the great angelic, prince who defends and has charge of your people. And there shall be time of trouble, straightness and distress such as never was since there was a nation till that time. But at whose name shall be found written in the Book of God's plan for His own. Daniel predicted in Chapter 12:1, the deliverance of translation of every saved Jew at the time the great tribulation begins for Israel. Daniel says everyone that shall be found written in the Book of Life among His people will be delivered from this great tribulation. The number of them written in the Book of Life is revealed in Revelation 7:1-8 and Revelation 14:1-5 How are they to be delivered from this tribulation except by rapture, if the woman and her remnant were saved at that time of the translation of 144,00 godly Jews they would also be translated, but the woman, or the nation as a whole, is not saved until three and half years (3 ½) later at the second advent Isaiah 66:7-8 Romans 11:25-29 The remnant turns to God after the catching up of the man child and after the catching up of the man child and after the prosecution and the flight of the woman into the wilderness (Revelation 12:17) therefore the 144,000 must be the man child. And the dragon was enraged with the woman, and he went to make war with the rest of her offspring, who keep the commandments of God and have the testimony of Jesus Christ

The Earthly Church Was Promised the City

According to the Gospel of (John Chapter 14:1-3) Do not let your hearts be troubled, distressed, agitated. You believe in and adhere to and trust in and rely on God, believe in and adhere to and trust in and rely also on me. In my father's house, there are many dwelling places, (homes) if it were not so, I would have told you, for I am going away to prepare a place for you. And when if I go and make ready a place for you, I will come back again and will take you to myself, that where I am you may be also. Jesus Christ the son of the Most High God when he was physically here on the Earth gave this important promise to the church that he would go back to His heavenly father, to prepare a place for His people. Hebrew 13:14 says, for here we have no continuing city, but we seek the one to come.

Every Christian is promised the city, He who overcomes, I will make him a pillar in the temple of My God, and he shall go out anymore. I will write on him the name of My God and the name of the New Jerusalem, which comes down out of Heaven from My God. And I will write on him a new name.

The Reasons Why One Hundred And Forty Four Thousand Are The Man Child.

Revelation 3:12 John 14:1-3 He-brew 12:22-22 But you have come to Mount Zion and to the city of the Living God, the heavenly Jerusalem, to an innumerable company of angels, to the general Assembly and church of the first born who are registered in heaven, to God the Judge of all, to the spirits of just men made perfect. The one hundred and forty four thousand saints of the Jew were promised to be in the city of Jerusalem in heaven. The tribulation saints will go there. The bible says in the book of Revelation 6:9-11 when he opened the fifth seal, I saw under the altar the souls who had been slain for the Word of God and for the testimony which they held. And they cried with a loud voice, saying, How long, O Lord, holy and true, until you judge and avenge our blood and those who dell on the Earth? Then a white robe was given to each of them, and it was said to them that they should rest a little while longer, until both the number of their fellow servants and their brethren, who would be killed as they were, was completed. A multitude of people from the Great Tribulation- After these things I looked, and behold, a great multitude which no one could number, of all nations, tribes, peoples and tongues, standing before the throne and before the lamb, clothed with white robes, with palm branches in their hands, and crying out with a loud voice, saying, salvation belongs to our God who sits on the throne, and the Lamb. All the angels stood around the throne, and the Lamb. All the angels stood around the throne and the elders and the four living creatures, fell on their faces before the throne and worshipped God, saying, Amen, Blessing and glory and wisdom, Thanksgiving and honor and power and might be to our God forever and ever, Amen. The book of Revelation 15:2-4 says, And I saw something like a sea of glass mingled with fire, and those who have the victory over the beast, over his image and over his mark and over the number of his name, standing on the sea of glass, having harps of God. They sing the song of Moses, the servant of God, and the Song of the Lamb, saying, great and marvelous are your works, Lord God Almighty. Just and true are your ways, King of the Saints, who shall not fear your, O Lord, and glorify your name? For you alone are holy. For all nations shall come and worship before you. For your judgments have been manifested.

    The Saints reign with Christ for one thousand years. And I saw thrones, and they sat on them, and judgment was committed to them. Then I saw the souls of those who had been beheaded for their witness to Jesus and for the word of God, who had not worshipped the beast or his image, and had not received his mark on their foreheads or on their hands. And they lived and reigned with Christ for a thousand years. But the rest of the dead did not live again until the thousand years were finished. This is the first resurrection. Blessed and holy is he who has part in the first resurrection. Over such the second has no power, but they shall be priests of God and of Christ, and shall reign with him a thousand years. Therefore we conclude that since all saints in the first resurrection from Abel to the last one saved in the future tribulation will go to live in the New Jerusalem that all such saints will be members of the bride, no one person, group of persons, denomination, mansion, temple or any other building can be called the City Lamb's wife. It is scriptural however to say concerning the redeemed, that they are now married to Christ under the terms of the New Covenant that they are citizens of heaven, that they have hope of going to live in the New Jerusalem, and because of this they expect to be a part of the bride of Christ or part of the heavenly City. But no one is actually a part of the bride until he begins to live in that beautiful city of New Jerusalem which is the bride, the Lamb's wife. (Revelation 21:9-10)

    The church who is the bride of Christ is now married. Jesus called himself the bridegroom of Christians. And Jesus said to them, Can the friends of the bridegroom mourn as long as the bridegroom is with them? But the days will come when the bridegroom will be taken away from them, and then they will fast. The Disciples of John the Baptist came to Jesus to ask him questions, saying, why do we and the Pharisees fast often, but your disciples do not fast, Jesus answered them that as far as the bridegroom is with the bride, they could not fast but when the groom is taken away from them then the bride and her friends will fast. When Jesus Christ after his death and resurrection, he was ascended into heaven, then the disciples of the Lord Jesus also fasted. When a bridegroom wed her bride and they went to the honey moon, they cannot go there and start fasting while people are there to serve them. John the Baptist called Jesus Christ the bridegroom. John 3:29 He who has the bride is the bridegroom, but the friend of the bridegroom, who stands and hears him, rejoices greatly because of the bridegroom's voice. Therefore, this joy of mine is fulfilled. Christians are married to God and Christ under terms of the New Testament and the Israel was married to God under the terms of the Old Testament Matthew 26:26-30 And as they were eating, Jesus took the bread, blessed and broke it and gave it to the disciples and said, Take, eat, this is my body. Then He took the cup, drink from it all of you. For this is my blood of the New Covenant which is shed for many for the remission of sins. But I say to you, I will not drink of this fruit of the vine from now on until that day when I drink it new with you in my Father's Kingdom, and when they had sung a hymn, they went out to the Mount Olives. Jesus Christ the Mediator of the New Covenant, and to the blood of sprinkling that speaks better things than the blood of Abel. Apostle Paul taught Christians are married to Christ Jesus by the New Covenant, see Romans 7:1-6 Or do you not know, brethren for I speak to those who know the Law, that the law has dominion over a man as long as he lives?

For the woman who has a husband is bound by the law to her husband as long as he lives. But if the husband dies, she is released from the law of her husband. So then, if while her husband lives, she marries another man, she will be called adulteress, but if the husband dies, she is free from the law, so that she is no adulteress, though she has married another man. Therefore, my brethren, you also have become dead to the law through the body of Christ, that you may be married to another to Him who was raised from the dead, that you should bear the fruit to God. For when we were in the flesh, the sinful passions which were aroused by the law were at work in our members to bear fruits to death. But now we have been delivered from the law, having died to what we were held by, so that we should serve in the newness of the Spirit and not in the oldness of the letter. Jesus revealed to use in Revelation 22:16-17 that I, Jesus, have sent my Messenger (angel) to you to witness and give you assurance of these things for the churches (assemblies) I am the Root (the source) and the offspring of Da-vid, the radiant and brilliant morning star (Isaiah 11:1-10) The Holy Spirit and the bride of the Christ, the true Christians says come. And let him who is listening say come. And let everyone come who is thirsty, (who is pain-fully conscious of his need of those things by which the soul is refreshed, supported and strengthened and whoever desires to do it, let him come, take, appropriate and drink water of life without cost. (Isaiah 55:1) This is an invitation to abundant life. Ho! Everyone who thirsts, come to the waters, and you who have no money, come, buy and eat. Yes, come buy wine and milk without money and without price. And he said to me, it is done, I am the Alpha and Omega, the Beginning and the End. I will give of the fountain of the water of life freely to him who thirsts. He who overcomes shall inherit all things, and I will be in his God and he shall be my son. The bible says in Isaiah 61:10 I will greatly rejoice in the Lord, my Soul shall be joyful in my God, for he has clothed me with the

The Reasons Why One Hundred And Forty Four Thousand Are The Man Child.

garments of salvation. He has covered me with the robe of righteousness, as a bridegroom decks himself with jewels.

Revelation 19:14-15 and the troops of heaven, clothed in fine linen, dazzling and clean, followed Him on white horses. Jude 1:14-15 Now Enoch, the seventh from Adam, prophesied about these men also, saying, behold the Lord comes with ten thousands of His saints. To execute judgment on all, to convict all who are ungodly among them of all their ungodly among them of all their ungodly deeds which they have committed in an ungodly way, and of all the harsh things which ungodly sinners have spoken against Him.

Daniel 7:9 I watched till thrones were put in place, and the Ancient of Days was seated. His garment was as white as snow. And the hail of His head was like pure wool. His throne was a fiery flame, its wheels a burning fire. A fiery stream issued and came forth from before Him. A thousand thousands ministered to Him, ten thousand times ten thousand stood before Him. The court was seated and the books were opened.

The Revelation of Jesus Christ, which God gave Him to show His servants things which must shortly take place? And he sent and signified it by His angels to His Servant John, who bore witness to the Word of God, and to the testimony of Jesus Christ, to all things that he saw. Blessed is he who reads and those who hear the Words of this prophecy, and keep those things which are written in it for the time is near.

Grace to you and peace to Him, who is and who was and who is to come and from the seven spirits who are before His throne, and from Jesus Christ, and from Jesus Christ the faithful witness, the firstborn from the dead, the ruler over the Kings of the Earth. To whom who loved us and washed us from our sins in His own blood. Read Ps 89:27-29 Says, also I will make Him my first born, the highest of the Kings of the Earth. My Mercy, I will keep from Him forever and My Covenant shall stand firm with him. His seed also I will make to endure forever. And His throne as the days of heaven. And has made us Kings and Priests to his God and Father, to him be glory and dominion forever and ever Amen.

Behold, He is coming with clouds, and every eye will see Him, even they who pierced Him. And all tribes of the Earth will mourn, because of Him, even so Amen. I am the Alpha and the Omega, the Beginning and the End says the Lord, who is ad who was and who is to come, the Almighty.

I, John, your brother and companion in the tribulation and the Kingdom and patience of Jesus Christ, was on the Island that is called Patmos for the word of God and the testimony of Jesus Christ. I was in the spirit on the Lord's day, and I head behind me a loud voice, as a trumpet, saying, I am the Alpha and the Omega, the First and the Last, and what you see, write the book and send it to the Seven Churches which are Asia, to Ephesus, to Smyrna, to Pergamum, to Thyatira, Sardis, to Philadelphia and to Laodicea. Then John turned to see the voice that spoke with him. And having turned I saw the seven golden lampstands and in the midst of the seven lampstands one like the Son of Man, clothed with a garment down to the feet and girded about the chest with a golden band. His head and hair were white like a wool, as white as snow, and His eye like a flame of fire. (Daniel 7:13-14) says I saw in the night visions and behold, on the clouds of the heavens came one like a son of man, and He came to the Ancient of Days and was presented before Him. And there was given Him (the Messiah) dominion and glory kingdom that all peoples, nations and languages should serve Him. His dominion is an everlasting dominion which shall not pass away, and His Kingdom is one of which shall not be destroyed.

The book of Revelation Chapter 5:1-10 confirmed what Daniel saw. And I saw in the right hand of Him who sat on the throne a scroll written inside and on the back, sealed with seven seals. Then I saw a strong angel proclaiming with loud voice, who is worth to open the scroll and to lose its seals? And no one in heaven or on the earth or under the earth was able to open the scroll, or to look at it, so I wept much, because no one was found worthy to open and read the scroll, or look at it. But one of the elders said to me. Do not weep. Behold, the Lion of the tribe of Judah, the Root of David has prevailed to open the scroll and lose its seven seals. And I looked, and behold, in the midst of the throne and the four living creatures, and in the midst of the elders, stood a Lamb as though it had been slain, having seven horns and seven eyes, which the seven Spirits of God are sent out in all the Earth. Then He came and took the scroll out of the ri8ght hand of Him who sat on the throne. Now when He had taken the scroll, the four living creatures and the twenty four elders fell down before the Lamb, each having a harp, and golden bowls full of Incense, which are the prayers of the saints.

And they sand a new song, saying, you are worthy to take the scroll. And to open its seals, for you were slain, and have redeemed us to God by your blood out of every tribe and tongue and people and nation, and have made us Kings and Priests to our God, and we shall reign on the EARTH. Daniel 10:5 says I lifted my eyes and looked, and behold a man clothed in linen, whose loins were girded with pure gold of phase.

In Revelation Chapter 1:14 John saw His head and His hair were white like white wool, as snow, and His eyes like a flame of fire. Daniel 7:9 tell us the vision of the Ancient of Days, I watched till thrones were put in place, and the Ancient of Days was seated, His garment was as white as snow. And the hair of His head was like pure wool. His throne was a fiery flame, its wheels a burning fire.

His feet were like fine brass, as if refined in a furnace, and His voice as the sound of many waters. Daniel Chapter 10:6 says His body was like beryl, his face like the appearance of lightning, his eyes like touches of fire, his arms and feet like burnished bronze in color, and the sound of his words like the voice of multitude. In His right hand He held seven stars, and from His mouth there came forth a sharp two edged sword, and His face was like the sun shining in full power at midday. The book of Exodus 34:29-30 says when Moses came down from Sinai with the two tables of the Testimony in his hand, he did not know that the body of his skin of his face shone and sent forth beams by reason of his speaking with the Lord. And when Aaron and all the Israelites looked at Moses and saw his face shining, they were afraid to come near him.

Reasons Why One Forty Four Thousand Are the Man Child

1. It has been proven that the sun clothed woman is the national Israel. The man child then could not be either the Gentiles or the Church which is made up mainly of Gentiles. (Acts 15:13-18) And after they had become silent, James answered, saying, Men and brethren, listen to me, Simon he declared how God at the first visited the Gentiles to take out of them a people for His name. And with this the words of the prophets agree, just as it is written. After this I will return and will rebuild the tabernacle of David, which has fallen down, I will rebuild its ruins. And I will set it up, so that the rest of mankind may seek the Lord, says the Lord who does all these things. Known to God from eternity are all His works. The woman would have to produce of her own kind according to the Law of Reproduction given by God (Genesis chapter 1:22-28) Therefore if the woman is Jewish the man-child must also be Jewish. The woman represent a company of people. There is no other company in the event of Revelation chapter 4-19 that could possibly be symbolized by the man-child other than 144,000 Jesus of Revelation chapter 7 and 14.
2. The man child cannot me Christ because everything from Revelation 4:1 on must be after the churches of Rev 2:1 to

The Reasons Why One Hundred And Forty Four Thousand Are The Man Child.

Revelation 3:22 How could John see the historical ascension of Christ as happening among the things to be in the middle of Daniel's 70th week of 3 ½ years before the second advent of Christ.

3. The man-child cannot be the Church as a whole, or in part, as some teach, because the church is raptured in Rev 4:1 before the events of Rev 4-22 which must be after the churches.

4. The man-child represents a company of all living people who will be translated without seeing death, the woman brings forth either a dead or a living child, not one partly dead or not one partly alive, the dragon could not one already dead at birth (Rev 12:4) The child is caught up to God alive as soon as it is born (Revelation 12:4-5) The 144,000 which must be after the churches, that could possibly be the man-child whose life the dragon tries to take (Revelation 7:1-8, 14:1) Since the O.T. Saints and the Church Saints are all resurrected to immortality by this time, it would be impossible for the dragon to kill them.

5. Revelation 7:1-8, 14:1-5, 9:4 give a complete revelation of the 144,000 their number, Salvation, sealing in the forehead, protection through the first six trumpets, rapture under the seven trumpet as the man-child, and their destiny and position, in heaven after their rapture. If one of these passages is taken away the revelation about them is incomplete. We have them on Earth all through the first six trumpets. Revelation 7:1-3, 9:4 and in heaven immediately after the catching up of the man-child in the 7th trumpet. Revelation 14: 1-5 So if they are not the man-child who is he and how did the 144,000 are before God's throne in heaven, having been redeemed from the Earth and from among men. They are in heavenly people that last 3 ½ years of tribulation is identical with that of the man-child. (Rev 12:5)

6. The time of the Rapture of the 144,000 proves them to be the man-child. The time of their translation is identical with that of the man-child. Revelation 12:5, 14:1-5

7. We have seen that the Church and the O.T. Saints are to be raptured before Daniel's 70th week and the tribulation. We have seen that the great multitude of tribulation Saints will be killed mainly after and raptured after the 144,000 in heaven (Rev 6:9-11 7:9-17) The only other company caught up beside these is the 144,000 and only place the rapture (Rev 12:5) Therefore the man-child and the 144,000 must be the same. If they are not the same, then we do not know whom the man-child represents or how the 144,000 gets to heaven. Where is the revelation of their rapture if it is not in Revelation 12:5?

8. The place where the `144,000 saints are, in the book of Revelation 14:1-5 proves they will be in heaven during the last three and half years of the tribulation, so they must be raptured before then, when, if not as the man-child? The Mount Zion is the heavenly one (see Hebrews, Chapter 12:22-24) But you have come to Mount Zion and to the City of the Living God, the heavenly Jerusalem, to an innumerable company of angels to the generals assembly and Church of the firstborn who are registered in heaven, to God the Judge of all, to the Spirits of Just men made perfect, to Jesus the Mediator of the New Covenant, and to the blood of sprinkling that speaks better things than that of Abel. (Revelation 14:1-2) Then I looked, and behold the Lamb stood on Mount Zion, and with him 144,000 men who had His name and His Father's name inscribed on their foreheads. And I heard a voice from heaven like the sound of great waters and like the ramblings of mighty thunder, the voice I heard seemed like the music of harpist accompanying themselves on their harps.

9. The 144,000 are the first fruits to God from Israel after the rapture of every saved Jews and Gentiles of after the Church in Revelation 4:1 They are not saved when the Church is raptured or they would go up also, I Thessalonians 4:16 For the Lord Himself will descend from heaven with shout, with the voice of an arch angel, and with the trumpet of God. And the dead in

The Reasons Why One Hundred And Forty Four Thousand Are The Man Child.

Christ will rise first. Then we who are alive and remain shall be caught up together with them in the cloud to meet the Lord in the air. And thus we shall always be with the Lord. But each in his own rank and turn, Christ the Messiah is the first fruits, then those who are Christ's Own will be resurrected at His coming. (I Corinthians 15:23) Since they are saved after that in the first 3 ½ years of the tribulation, their tribulation must be the same as that of the man-child, which represent a company of the Jews from Israel, were to be saved and raptured before the 144,000 then the man-child will be first fruits to God from Israel and not the 144,000. But since the 144,000 are to be the first fruits, then it is clear that they are the first Jews saved and raptured from Israel during the tribulation of 7 years between the rapture of the Church and the Second Advent. This proves that the 144,000 are the ones symbolized by the man-child.

There is only one company saved and raptured between the rapture of the church at the beginning of Daniel seventy week (70th week) and the rapture of the tribulation saints at the end of this week. The company is symbolized by the man-child and clearly revealed to be 144,000 Jews (Rev 7:1-8, 9:4, 12:5 Revelation 14:1-5) The 144,00 are specifically sealed for protection to go through the trumpet judgments only immediately after the seventh (7th) trumpet, which include all Revelation chapter 11:15 and 13:18 we see the 144,000 in heaven (Revelation 14:1)

10. Then I looked, and behold, a lamb standing on Mount Zion, and with Him one hundred and forty-four thousand, having His father's name written on their foreheads. And I heard a voice of many waters, and like the voice of loud thunder. And I heard sound of harpists playing their harps. They sang as it were a new song be-fore the throne, before the four living creatures, and before the elders, and no one could learn that song except the hundred and forty-four thousand who were redeemed from the Earth. These are the ones who were not defiled with women,

for they are virgins. These are the ones who follow the Lamb wherever He goes. These were redeemed from among men, being first fruits to God and to the Lamb. And in their mouth was found no deceit, for they are without fault before the Throne of God. They were spotless, untainted, without blemish, before the throne of God. The way God protects them from the wrath of Satan under the seventh (7th) trumpet is by catching them up to God and His throne. The woman, man-child and remnant of the woman are the only Jewish Companies in the (Revelation chapter 12:1-2, 5 and 17) The 144,000 must be one of these three companies, for they are sealed out of all tribes of the Children of Israel (see Revelation 7:1-8) They are in no place mentioned separately from those three companies as a forth company and there is no indication of them as such, since they are one of the three companies, which one? They cannot be the woman or the remnant for these remain on Earth while the 144,000 are translated (Rev 14:1-5)

The 144,000 therefore must be the man-child. The 144,000 are the only one that could possibly fulfill the statement about man-child in Revelation 12. The man-child and the 144,000 represents a small company (Revelation 7:1-9) They both are caught up to God and throne (12:5) and Revelation 14:1-5 they both are delivered from the wrath of the dragon (Rev 12:4-5) and they both are in heavenly people, so must be the same company. Prophet Isaiah chapter 66:7-8 says before she was in labor, she gave birth, before her pain came, and she delivered a male child. Who has heard such a thing? Who has seen such a thing? Shall the Earth be made to give birth in one day? Or Zion was in labor, she gave birth to her children. The Prophet predicts Israel as bringing forth the man-child before she is delivered or saved at the end of the tribulation (Zechariah 12:10-14) And I will pour on the house of David and on the inhabitants of Jerusalem the spirit of grace and supplication, yes, they will mourn for Him as one mourns for his only son, and grave for Him as one grieves for a firstborn. In that day, there shall be a great mourning in Jerusalem, like the mourning at Hadad Rimmon in the pain of Megiddo. And the land shall mourn, every family by itself, and their wives by themselves, the family of the house of Levi by itself, and their wives by themselves, the family of Shimei by itself, and their wives by themselves. All the family that remain, every family by itself, and their wives by themselves. Romans 11:25-29 God, through Apostle Paul tells us that, For I do not desire, brethren, that you should be ignorant of this mystery, lest you be wise in your opinion, that blindness in part has happened to Israel until the fullness of the Gentiles has come in. And so all Israel will be saved, as it is written, The Deliverer will come out Zion, and He will turn away ungodliness from Jacob, for this is My Covenant with them, when I take away their sings. Concerning the gospel they are enemies for your sake, but concerning the election they are beloved for the sake of the fathers. For the gifts and the calling of God are irrevocable.   Who is the man-child that Israel is to bring forth before her own conversion at the Second Advent if not the 144,000 of Rev 14:1-5 And Revelation 7:1-8 Daniel chapter 12:1 The Bible says, And at that time of the end Michael shall arise, the great angelic, prince who defends and has charge of your people. And there shall be time of trouble, straightness and distress such as never was since there was a nation till that time. But at whose name shall be found written in the Book of God's plan for His own. Daniel predicted in Chapter 12:1, the deliverance of translation of every saved Jew at the time the great tribulation begins for Israel. Daniel says everyone that shall be found written in the Book of Life among His people will be delivered from this great tribulation. The number of them written in the Book of Life is revealed in Revelation 7:1-8 and Revelation 14:1-5 How are they to be delivered from this tribulation except by rapture, if the woman and her remnant were saved at that time of the translation of 144,00 godly Jews they would also be translated, but the woman, or the nation as a whole, is not saved until three and half years (3 ½) later at the second advent Isaiah 66:7-8 Romans 11:25-29 The remnant turns to God after the catching up of the man-child and after the catching up of the man-child and after the prosecution and the flight of the woman into the wilderness (Revelation 12:17) therefore the 144,000 must be the man-child. And the dragon was enraged with the woman, and he went to make war with the rest of her offspring, who keep the commandments of God and have the testimony of Jesus Christ.

Chapter Twenty
Will The Rapture Of The Church Happen First Before The Reveal Of The Antichrist?

Deceptions: According to Random House Webster's College Dictionary define deception as the act of deceiving, or the state of being deceived, something that deceives or is intended to deceive. Jesus answered them, be careful that no one misleads you, deceiving you and leading you into error. For many will come in on the strength of my name appropriating the name which belongs to me, saying, I am the Christ the Messiah, and they will lead many astray. And many false prophets will rise up and deceive and lead many into error. For false Christ's and false prophets will arise, and they will show great signs and wonders so as to deceive and lead astray, if possible, even the elect God's Chosen Ones. The Bible tells us in I John 4:1-3 Beloved, do not believe every spirit, but test the spirits whether they are of God, because many false prophets have gone out into the world. By this you know the Spirit of God, Every spirit that confesses that Jesus Christ has come in the flesh is of God and every spirit that does not confess that Jesus Christ has come in the flesh is not of God. And this is the Spirit of an Antichrist, which you have heard was coming, and is now already in the world. Jesus said in John 5:43 I have come in My Father's name and you do not receive me, if another comes in his own name, him you will receive. But also in those days, there arose false prophets among the people, just as there will be false teachers among yourselves, who will subtly and stealthily introduce heretical doctrines, destructive heresies, even denying and disowning the Master who brought them, bringing upon themselves swift destruction. And many will follow their destructive ways, because of whom the way of the truth will be blasphemed.

2 Peter 2:1-2 states, "Then I saw an angel standing in the sun and cried with a loud voice, saying to all the birds that fly in the midst of heaven, come and gather together for the supper of the great God, that you may eat the flesh of the Kings, the flesh of Captains the flesh of mighty men, and the flesh of all people, free and slave, both small and great, And I saw the beast, the Kings of the Earth, and the armies, gathered together to make war against Him who sat on the horse and against His army. Then the beast was captured, and with him the false prophet who worked signs in his presence, by which he deceived those who received the mark of the beast and those who worshipped his image. These two were cast alive into the lake of fire burning with brimstone. Rev 19:17-20 Now the spirit expressly says that in latter times some will depart from the faith, giving heed to deceiving spirits and doctrines of demons speaking lies in hypocrisy, having own conscience seared with a hot iron. Forbidding to marry, and commanding to abstain from food which God created to be received with Thanksgiving by those who believe and know the truth. (I Timothy 4:1-3)

Then Jesus said to him, unless you see signs and wonder (miracles) happen, you people will not believe trust and have faith at all. Jesus is giving us a picture here that many will go after miracles God's miracles is real, beside that devil and his demons the false prophet will also work sign and miracles in the presence of the beast to deceived many people to their destruction, this is why Jesus is telling us to be watchful so that no one could deceive us.

Who Are the False Christ's Prophets?

For many will come in my name, saying I am the Christ and will deceive many. And if anyone says to you, look here is the Christ or there do not believe it. For false Christ's and false prophets will rise and show signs and wonder to deceive, if possible, even the elect? See, I have told you beforehand. Therefore, if they say to you, He is in the desert, do not go out, or look, He is in the inner rooms, do not believe it. According to John 4:48 Jesus said except you see signs and wonders you will not believe. The disciples of Jesus asked for the sign of his coming and the end of the age, Jesus first response was watch out that no one deceives you. The fact is that whenever we look for signs we become very susceptible to being deceived. There are many false prophets around with counterfeit signs, of spiritual power and authority. The only sure way to keep from being deceived is to focus on Christ and his words. Don't look for special signs and don't spend time looking at other people, look at Christ. You may facing intense persecution now but Christians in other parts of the world are. As you hear about Christians suffering for their faith you must know that they are your brothers and sisters in Christ. The Old Testament frequently mentions false prophets. Prophet Elisha said to the King of Israel, what do we have to do with each other? Go to the prophets of your father and the prophets of your mother. Jehoshaphat's requested for a prophet of the Lord, show how true worship and religious experience in both Israel and Judah had declined. In David's day both high priest and the prophets gave the King advice. But most of the priests had left Israel and God's prophets were seen as messengers of doom. This miracle predicted by Elisha affirmed Gods power and authority and validated Elisha's ministry. King Jehoshaphat of Judah and King Ahab of Israel gave the prophet Micaiah a similar request but they ignored Gods advice, with disastrous results. Then Micaiah answered, I saw all Israel scattered on the hills like sheep without shepherd and the Lord said, these people have no master. Let each one go home in peace. The King of Israel said to Jehoshaphat, didn't I tell you that he never prophesies anything good about me, but only bad. Micah continued, therefore hear the word of the Lord, I saw the Lord sitting on his throne with all the host of heaven standing around him on his right and on his left. And the Lord said who will entice Ahab into attacking Remoth Gilead and going to his death there? Then Zedekiah son of Keneanah went up and slapped Micah in the face. Which way did the spirit from the Lord ho when he went from me to speak to you? He asked Micah replied, you will find out on the day you go to hide in an inner room.

The King of Israel then ordered take Micah and send him back to Ammon the ruler of prison and give him nothing but bread and water until I re-turn safely. Micah declared if you ever return safely, the Lord has not spoken through me then he added mark my words all the people. The vision Micah saw was either a picture of a real incident in heaven, or a parable of what was happening on Earth, illustrating that the seductive influence of the false prophets would be part of God's Judgment upon Ahab, whether or not God sent an Angel in disguise, he used the system of false prophet to snare Ahab in his sin. The lying spirit symbolized the way of life for those prophets who told the King only what he wanted to hear. The Bible shows us a God who hate all evil and will one day do away with it

Completely and forever. God does not entice anyone to become evil. Those committed to evil, however, may be used by God to sin even more in order to hurry their deserved Judgment. We don't need to understand every detail of how God works in order to have perfect confidence in his absolute power over evil and his total goodness toward us. Ahab could not escape God's Judgment. The King of Aram sent 32 of his best chariot commanders with the sole purpose of killing Ahab. Thinking he could escape, Ahab tried a disguise, but a random arrow struck him while the chariots chased the wrong King Jehoshaphat, it was foolish for Ahab to think he could escape by wearing a disguise, sometimes people try to escape reality by disguising themselves changing jobs, moving to a new town, even changing spouses. But God sees and evaluates the motives of each person any attempted disguise is futile. Just as the Prophet of God had predicted, Ahab was killed. False prophets claimed to receive messages from God, but they preached health and wealth messages. They said what the people wanted to hear, even when the nation was not following God as it should, when people are living in sinful attitude, walking in the flesh such as adultery, fornication, uncleanliness, lewdness or indecency, idolatry, sorcery, enmity, hatred, strife, jealousy, anger (ill temper) selfish ambitions, dissensions or divisions or party spirit, heresies, envy, murders, drunkenness, revelries, and the like of which I tell you beforehand, just as I also told you in time past, that those who practice such things will not inherit the Kingdom of God. God want his people to stay away from sinful attitude but instead of the prophets to tell them the truth in God's word for them to repent for their sin, the false prophets will tell them what they

    They will be happy so that they may have favor in the sight of the people, so that they will get money and other things from them, like King Ahab, he doesn't like the truth, he did what is evil, in the sight of God will not tell him what he wanted to hear, but rather what he don't want to hear, that was why King Ahab told Jehoshaphat to Micah did not prophesied anything good about him but rather bad, because God found out that King Ahab was an enemy of righteousness, so he like to inquired from the false prophets who will not tell him truth and counsel him to draw near to God, but rather prophesy prosperity, blessing, wealth, and praising those who are enemies of progress and righteousness. These prophets tell people who are in sin that God wants you to be rich, do whatever your desires tell you, and they say there is no hell, but I want to tell you today that hell is real all the disobedience people will found themselves in hell. Jesus said false teachers would come, and he warned his disciples as he warn us not to listen to their dangerous words. With false teachings and loose morals come a particularly destructive disease, the loss of true love for God and others. Sin cools your love for God and others by turning your focus on yourself. You cannot truly love if you think only of yourself. Jesus warning about the false teachers still hold true upon close examination it becomes clear that many nice sounding messages don't agree with God's message in the Bible. Only a solid foundation in God's message in the Bible. Only a solid foundation in God's word can equip us to perceive the errors and distortion in the false teaching, in our society today. And many false prophets will rise up and deceive and lead many into error. (Matthew 24:11) Jesus has open our eyes to know that many false prophets will come only to deceive people for them to deviate from the right part of God Almighty, so you supposed to be watchful by means of depending on the word of God and the Holy Spirit to direct you always. You must be watchful of the places where you go for your spiritual needs.

THE SIGNS OF THE TIME AND THE END OF THE AGE

While He was seated on the Mount of Olives, the disciples came to Him privately and said, Tell us, when will this take place, and what will be the signs of Your coming and the end of completion the consummation of this age? Jesus answered them, be careful that no one misleads you, deceiving you and lead you into error. The disciples of the Lord Jesus Christ came to Him on the Mount of Olives to asked the very important question, that every believer must to ask, tell us when will these things be, and what will be the sign of Your coming, and the end of the age. Every believer must know that one

day this world will come to an end, heaven is our final destination, we are strangers here on this earth, they asked Him, when are you coming again, Jesus said to them, take heed that no one deceives you. For many will come in my name and shall deceive many. –Matthew 24:1-5.
Today many are those who are out there to deceive people, there are false teachers, false Prophets, don't let anyone deceive you, Jesus is coming soon.

WILL THE RAPTURE OF THE CHURCH HAPPENS FIRST BEFORE THE REVEAL OF THE ANTICHRIST?

Let no man deceive you by any means, for the Day will not come unless the fallen away comes first, and the man of sin is revealed, the son of perdition, who opposes and exalts himself above all that is called God or that is worshiped, so that he sits as God in the temple of God, showing himself that he is God. 2 Thessalonians 2:3-4. It is obviously true that so many things will happen before the rapture of the Church and some people are also saying that the Antichrist will be reveal before the rapture of the Church, and this claim is false or not true, because the Scriptures clearly tell us that the fallen away will happen first, and the man of sin who is the Antichrist is revealed, Apostle Paul explained it clearly that we should be focus, that no one deceive us by any means for the Day of the Lord will not come unless the fallen away comes first. The King James version English phrase " fallen away " in 2 Thessalonians 2:3 is the one Greek word" Apostasia" is a compound of two Greek words Apo" to move away, Stasis means standing or state or to stand. From the basic definition, Apostasia means to go away from, or depart, or change state or standing from one state to another. Apostasia was used in extra Biblical Greek literature to describe political revolt, or going away from establishment in the Septuagint or Greek Old Testament, when the Jews would go away from God to worship other gods.

Apostasia is only used one other time in the New Testament, in the book of Acts to describe forsaking, or going away from the teachings of Moses. But they have been informed about you that you teach all the Jews who are among the Gentiles to forsake Moses, saying that they ought not to circumcise their children nor to walk according to the customs. Acts 21:21. Apostasy, which is noun form, appears in the book of Matthew 5:31, Matthew 19:7, and Mark 10:4 all these bible verses describes writing of divorcement, or papers that separate the man and woman, so that someone can go away from, and to go away from what must be determined. Falling away will definitely come first, the separating, taking away to meet the Lord in the air. In the book of 1 Thessalonians 4:13-18 But I do not want you be ignorant, brethren, concerning those who have fallen asleep, lest you sorrow as others who do not have hope.

For if we believe that Jesus died and rose again, even so God will bring with Him those who sleep in Christ Jesus. For this we say to you by the word of the Lord, that we who are alive and remain until the coming of the Lord will by no means proceed those who are asleep. For the Lord Himself will descend from heaven with a shout, with the voice of an archangel, and with the trumpet of God. And the dead in Christ will rise first, then we who are alive and remain shall be caught up together with them in the clouds to meet the Lord in the air. And thus shall we always be with the Lord. Therefore, comfort one another with these words

In the book of 1 Thessalonians 4:17 Scriptures tell me that we shall be caught up together, taking away separate from this world or earth to meet the Lord in the air, and the Holy Spirit will lead us, to illuminate us or transport us to the air to meet the Lord Jesus who will us to heaven. The Holy Spirit will not be on this earth by the time the Anti-Christ is revealed, The

Holy Spirit will be with the Church in heaven, now the Holy Spirit is the chief Executive of the Church, because this is His dispensation till He lead us to heaven, then Holy Spirit will finish His work, whereby Christ Jesus will marry the Church, then gifts will be giving to each and every one according to what we came here on this earth to do and the Lord will eat the last communion with us in heaven, the same seven years that the Church will be in heaven, the Anti-Christ will take control of this earth for seven years likewise the Anti-Christ will introduce the money which the whole earth is going to use which is six hundred and sixty six (666) Revelation 13:16-18 He causes all, both small and great, rich and poor, free and slave, to receive a mark on their right hand or on their foreheads, and that no one may buy or sell except one who has the mark or the name of the beast, or the number of his name. Here is wisdom. Let him who has understanding calculate the number of the beast, for it is the number of a man, his number is 666.

The only person through Him while the Anti-Christ is not revealed is the Holy Spirit, He cannot be with the son of perdition, the man of sin or the Anti-Christ at the same time and as far as the Church is not rapture the Holy Spirit will be on this earth until the Church is raptured then the son of perdition will be revealed.

God has done it before when He wanted to destroyed Sodom and Gomorrah, He did not destroyed the righteous people and the sinners together, God sent His angels to move the righteous man Lot and his family before the city was destroyed, snatched them out from Sodom before the destruction Genesis 19:15-19 .

Jesus said that likewise during the days of Noah whom God found him righteous person, He asked Noah to prepared an ark, Noah preached one hundred and twenty years but the people did not obey to the servant of God, he made the ark but people refused to go inside the Ark, only eight people entered into the Ark, Noah's and his family only they were eight in number after they entered into the ark, there was rainfall which destroyed the whole world in Noah's time.

God saw Noah as a righteous man, He did not destroyed him with the disobedient people but rather save Noah and his family, likewise the rapture of the Church will come first before the Anti-Christ is revealed.

For the mystery of the lawlessness, that hidden the principle of rebellion against constituted authority, is already at work in the world, but it is restrained only until He who is restrains is taken out of the way, And then the lawless one, the anti-Christ will be revealed and the Lord Jesus will slay him with the breath of His mouth and bring him to an end, by His appearing at His second coming 2 Thessalonians 2:7-8. The Holy Spirit is the hinderer of this passage, the Scripture used the word pronoun and capital letter He, personal pronoun it is believed that the Church could not be referred to as He, because the Church is the bride of Christ Jesus. The Church is spoken of as a virgin, a woman, and is referred to as a pronoun her. But with righteousness He shall judge the poor, and decide with equity of the meek of the earth, and shall strike the earth with a rod of His mouth, and with the breath of His lips He shall slayed the wicked. Isaiah 11:4 The Holy Spirit will continue to hinder the lawlessness until the rapture of the Church, then the Antichrist will be revealed. This is conclusive proof that the rapture takes place before Prophet Daniel seventy (70th) week of years and the tribulation of Revelation chapter 6:1-2 Then I saw as a Lamb broke open one of the seven seals, and as if in a voice of thunder, I heard one of the four living creatures call out. And I looked, and saw there a white horse whose rider carried a bow. And a crown was given him, and he rode forth conquering and to conquer.

The one sitting on the white horse rider who carried a bow here is not Jesus the Messiah but the Antichrist. And when

He broke the second seal, I heard the second living creature call out come, and another horse came out flaming red and its rider was empowered to take the peace from the earth, so that men slaughter one another and he was given huge sword.

According to the book of Daniel chapter 9:27 The bible says, then he shall confirm a covenant with many for one week, but in the middle of the week he shall bring an end to sacrifice and offerings. And on the wing of abomination shall be one who make desolate. Even until consummation, which is determined is poured out on desolate according to Daniel 9:27 the word of God teaches even, days that the Antichrist will be on this earth is one week of years, one week of days is seven days, therefore one week of years is seven years(7years). The same seven years that the believers both dead and living will be rapture from this earth and reside in heaven, that same seven years the antichrist will also take control on this earth. Three things will happen to believers when we raptured in heaven.

1. The Lord Jesus will judge the works of believers, the judgment of believers is different from that of the unbelievers, you have make heaven but every ones work will definitely pass through fire.

2. The Lord Jesus will reward every believer according to what we came to this earth to do. Some believers will receive gold, some silver, others precious stone, wood, hay, and straw. The bible says in the book of (1s Corinthians chapter 3:12-13) But if anyone builds upon the Foundation whether it be with gold, silver, precious stones, wood, hay, straw. The work of each one will become plainly, openly, known, shown, for what it is for the day will declare it because it will be revealed by fire, the fire will test each one's work, of what sort it is.

3. The Lord Jesus Christ will eat the last supper with the believers in heaven, as He promised the disciples that He will not eat the communion or the supper, until it happens in heaven. But I say to you, I will not drink of this fruit of vine

from now on until that day when I drink it new with you in My Father's kingdom. Matthew 26:29. Jesus is now in heaven, all believers will join Him in heaven and there He will eat the Lord's Supper with the children of God in heaven.

After this I saw in the night visions, and behold, a fourth beast, dreadful and terrible, exceedingly strong. It huge iron teeth, it was devouring, breaking in pieces, and trampling and residue with its feet. It was different from all the beasts that was before it, and it had ten horns. I was considering the horns, and there was another horn, a little one, coming up among them, before whom three of the first horns were plucked out by the root. And there, in this horn, were eyes like the eyes of a man, and a mouth speaking pompous words.

The three of the first horns were uprooted before it. This could either be referring to a bloody conflict that will destroy three nations or region or confederacy, that opposes the Antichrist taking over power of global government.

While Daniel was thinking about the vision of King Nebuchadnezzar's dream he saw something new, little horn, an eleventh king, a man, will rise up among the nations of original ten kings. The little horn the Antichrist will subdue three of the kings and destroy their political power. Seven survival kings of the original ten (10 nations will submit to the domination of the little horn. This earthly leader will begin his role as Antichrist and world dictator. Apostle John's vision of a great beast arising from the Gentile nations, see Revelation 13:1-4 Then I stood on the sand of the sea, I saw a beast rising up out of the sea, having seven heads and ten horns and on his horns ten crowns, and his heads a blasphemous name. Now the beast which I saw was like a leopard, his feet were like feet of a bear, and his mouth like a mouth of a lion. The dragon gave him power, his throne, and great authority. And I saw one of his heads as if it had been mortally wounded, and his deadly wound was healed. And all the world marveled and followed the beast so they worshiped the dragon who gave the authority to the beast, they worship the beast, saying, who is like the beast? Who is able to make war with him? In the book of Daniel 7:2-8 Daniel spoke saying, I saw in my vision by night, and behold, and the four winds of heaven were stirring up the great sea. And four great beasts came up from the sea, each different from the other. The first was like a lion, and had eagle's wings. I watched till its wings were plucked off, and it was lifted up from the earth and made to stand on the two feet like a man, and the man heart was given to it. And suddenly another beast, a second like a bear. It was raised up on one side, and had three ribs in its mouth between its teeth. And they said thus to it, Arise, devour much flesh. After this I looked, and there was another, like a leopard, which had on its back four wings of a bird the beast also had four heads and dominion was given to it. Apostle John saw seven heads corresponding to the original ten leaders Daniel saw, including the three that had been pulled out by the roots, by the antichrist. Daniel 7:8 the ten crowns represent the ten kingdoms. In the book of Revelation 13:1 The horn that arose from the midst of the ten and disposed three is a single individual, He shall speak out see Daniel 7:25 He shall speak pompous words against the Most High, and shall intend to change times and law.

Daniel 8:24-25 states, "His power shall be mighty, but not by his own, he shall destroy fearfully, and shall prosper and thrive, He shall destroy the mighty, and also the holy people. Through his cunning, he shall cause deceit to prosper under his rule and he shall exalt himself in his heart. He shall destroy many in their prosperity, he shall even rise against the Prince of peace."

ANTICHRIST FALLACIES

And the ten horns out of this kingdom are ten kings that shall arise, and another shall arise after them, and he shall be diverse from the first, and he shall subdue three kings (Daniel 7:24). And I stood upon the sand of the sea, and saw, a beast rise up out of the sea, having seven heads and ten horns, and upon his horns ten crowns, and upon his heads the name of blasphemy. (Revelation 13:1)

1. That Antichrist will revive the Roman and reign from Rome is false. The Roman Empire will never be revived, nor will Antichrist have a part in the formation of the ten kingdoms inside the Roman Empire territory. He is to come after them, and not before them. See Daniel 7:23-24

2. That Antichrist will come from Rome and Italy is false. He will come from Babylon and future enlarged Syria. And out of one came of them came forth a little horn, which waxed exceeding great, toward the south, and toward the east, and toward the pleasant land. And it waxed great, even to the host of heaven, and it cast down some of the host and of the stars to the ground, and stamped upon them. The ram which thou saw having two horns are the king of Media and Persia. And the rough goat is the king of Grecian and the goat horn that is between his eyes is the first king. Now that being broken, whereas four stood up for it, four kingdoms shall stand up out of the nation, but not in his power. And in the latter time of their kingdom, when the transgressors are come to the full, a king of fierce countenance, and understanding dark sentences, shall stand up (Daniel 8:9-10, 20-23). See Daniel 11:35-45.

3. That Antichrist will be Nimrod, Antiochus Epiphanies, or any Egyptian, Assyrian, Babylonian, Medo-Persian, Grecian, or Roman king of the ancient past is false. He is not to be any resurrected man of the past, for he will be slain by Christ at Armageddon which means he will be a mortal man.

4. That Antichrist will be Mussolini, Hitler, Stalin, the Pope of Rome, or some other man who has recently lived is false. None of these men have come from Syria and some are not from the Roman Empire territory at all as is true of Antichrist. That one

of these recent men will be resurrected as the Antichrist is as false.

5. That Antichrist will be Judas Iscariot because both are called son of perdition is false.

6. That the Antichrist will be present magician from Syria is false. Antichrist will not be revealed or come into prominence in any sense until after the ten kingdoms are formed and until after the rapture of the Church

7. That Antichrist will be any man now prominent in the world affairs is false.

8. That Antichrist will be a child of the devil, a direct offspring of Satan, imitating incarnation of God in the flesh is false.

9. That Antichrist will be an incarnation of Satan is false. Satan is symbolized by the dragon (Revelation 12:9). And the great dragon was cast out, that old Serpent, called the Devil, and Satan, which deceived the whole world, he was cast out into the earth, and his angels were cast out with him. Who will give his power to the beast or the Antichrist? (2 Thessalonians 2:8-12)

John the beloved the Apostle of our Lord Jesus Christ said and I saw an angel come down from heaven, having the key of the bottomless pit and a great chain in his hand. And he laid hold on the dragon, that old serpent, which is the Devil and Satan, and bound him a thousand years, and cast him into the bottomless pit, and shut him, and set a seal upon him, that he should deceive the nation no more, till the thousand years should be fulfilled, and after that he must be loosed a little season. Revelation 20:1-3.)

According to what God revealed to his servant John, that a day is coming where by Satan would be bound and keep him in prison for one thousand years. And when the thousand years are expired, Satan shall be loosed out of his prison. And shall go out to deceive the nations which are in the four quarters of the earth, Gog and Magog, to gather them together to battle the number of whom is as the sand of the sea. And they went up on the breadth of the earth, and compassed the camp of the saints round about, and the beloved city, and fire came down from God out of heaven, and devoured them. And the devil that deceived them was cast into the lake of fire and brimstone, where the beast and the false prophet are, and shall be tormented day and night for ever and ever. And I saw a great white throne, and him that sat on it, from whose face the earth and the heaven fled away, and there was no place found for them. And I saw the dead, small and great, stand before God, and the books were opened, and another book was opened, which is the book of life, and the dead were judged out of those things which were written in the books, according to their works. And the sea gave up the dead which were in it, and the death and hell delivered up the dead which were them, and they were judged every one according to their works. And death and hell were cast into the lake of fire, this is the second death.

And whosoever was not found written in the book of life was cast into the lake of fire.

About the Author

Bishop Emmanuel Boachie is the General Overseer of Jesus Power Redemption Ministry and New Covenant Life Chapel Worldwide Bishop was one of the pioneers who started Garden City Commercial College, and was working as an accountant before he received the call of God as a Pastor in the year 1981. Bishop Boachie is called to be an Architect and a Builder and this is an apostolic office. Bishop was trained in the Redeemed Christian Bible College, and also continued his theological college at Shiloh Bible Training Centre for Pastors. Bishop is a standing member of the International Council of Churches and ministers of Great Britain, he is also a member of Ghanaian Ministers Fellowship International and he is the financial secretary of the Ministers association in New York, United States of America. Bishop is also a standing member of the Faithful Ministers Fellowship that is also a group of ministers of the gospel of the kingdom of God, in the State of New York, United States of America. Bishop Emmanuel is married to Mrs. Deborah Boachie, he is a husband of one wife, and God has bless him with five children, Pastor Richard Amoah, Mrs. Rachael Amoah, Rev, Enos Opoku Boateng, Mrs. Priscilla Ofori, Edmund Donkor and Emmanuelle Pomaah Boachie. Bishop usually preaches in trains, buses, and ferries, telling people to repent and come to Jesus Christ to receive the salvation of God and the Second coming of Jesus Christ. Bishop is a very faithful man in the service of God, a man of integrity, he is an anointed man of God, he has set himself apart as a man, who knows God and loves to obey Him all the time. His first book is called Freedom from Demonic Powers

Will The Rapture Of The Church Happen First Before The Reveal Of The Antichrist?.